98 High-Protein Lunches: Quick and Delicious Recipes for Busy Lives

HighProtein Lunches Quick

Contents

4

INTRODU(

Are you searching for delicious l
can whip up in no time? Look no further
Protein Lunches: Quick and Delicious Recipes for Busy Lives! This
cookbook provides delicious, simple recipes that you can prepare in no
time at all, without sacrificing the high-protein nutrition you need to
keep you feeling energized and satisfied throughout the day.

Whether you're a busy professional, a stay-at-home parent, a student or
simply someone who likes to stay fueled, this book is perfect for you.
With 98 recipes featuring quick and easy-to-follow instructions, it caters
to various skill levels — from beginners to advanced cooks. You can
choose from a variety of proteins, from lean ground beef to tofu, as well
as an array of tasty vegetables and whole grains.

Each of these recipes contain a healthy balance of protein, fat, and
carbohydrates to help you feel full, energized, and satisfied. Protein is
important for building muscle, maintaining a healthy weight, and
boosting your immune system. So get ready to start cooking a variety of
mouthwatering high-protein lunches that don't require extensive
preparation, time, or energy. Not to mention, these recipes are also
incredibly satisfying, delicious, and budget friendly.

Start your journey to more balanced meals with Cookbook 98 High-
Protein Lunches: Quick and Delicious Recipes for Busy Lives! Preparing
healthy, high-protein meals in a snap has never been easier— you can
easily satisfy your appetite with the help of this amazing cookbook. From
nutritious sandwiches to colorful salads and succulent stir-fries, you're
guaranteed to find numerous recipes that are incredibly delicious and
incredibly easy to make. Whether you're looking for a more traditional
lunch or trying something different and unique, this cookbook offers
plenty of options for you to explore.

So, let's get cooking! With the help of Cookbook 98 High-Protein
Lunches: Quick and Delicious Recipes for Busy Lives, you can
experience all the benefits that come from having nutrient-dense meals.
Whether you're looking for something that is light, delicious, and packed
with protein or something a little heartier and satisfying, you'll find
plenty of recipes to choose from. Get ready to say goodbye to those
boring and unhealthy lunches and hello to these flavorful and nutritious
high-protein recipes!

1. Zucchini Noodle Bowl with Peanut SauceQuinoa and Chickpea Salad

This vibrant and delicious Zucchini Noodle Bowl with Peanut Sauce and Quinoa Chickpea Salad is the perfect meal for a healthy and satisfying lunch or dinner. The bold flavours of a creamy peanut sauce and zesty zucchini noodles are balanced out by the crunchy and nutritious quinoa and chickpea salad.

Serving: 6

| Preparation Time: 10 minutes
| Ready Time: 10 minutes

Ingredients:
- 2 large zucchinis, spiralized
- 2 tablespoons sesame oil
- 2 cloves garlic, minced
- 2 tablespoons ginger, minced
- 2 tablespoons peanut butter
- 2 tablespoons lime juice
- 2 tablespoons soy sauce
- 2 tablespoons sesame seeds
- 2 tablespoons honey
- 1/2 cup cooked quinoa
- 1 cup cooked chickpeas
- 1/2 cup shredded red cabbage
- 1/2 cup diced red bell pepper
- 1/4 cup chopped fresh cilantro
- 1 tablespoon sesame oil

Instructions:
1. Heat a large wok or frying pan over medium heat.
2. Add sesame oil and then add garlic and ginger followed by zucchini noodles, stirring until noodles are tender, about 5 minutes.
3. Meanwhile, combine peanut butter, lime juice, soy sauce, sesame seeds and honey to make the peanut sauce.
4. In a large bowl, combine cooked quinoa and chickpeas with shredded red cabbage, red bell pepper and cilantro. Toss with sesame oil.
5. Divide noodles amongst desired plates and top with quinoa and chickpea salad. Drizzle with desired amount of peanut sauce.

Nutrition Information:
Calories: 320; Total Fat: 15g; Saturated Fat: 3g; Sodium: 434mg;
Carbohydrates: 36g; Fiber: 7g; Sugar: 12g; Protein: 11g

2. Lentil and Kale Soup

Lentil and Kale Soup is a nutritious and flavorful meal that can be
prepared in no time. This vegan-friendly, one pot soup is full of protein,
fiber, and vitamins that make it an ideal simple dinner or lunch.
Serving: 4
| Preparation Time: 15 minutes
| Ready Time: 35 minutes

Ingredients:
• 2 tablespoons olive oil
• 2 carrots, chopped
• 1 onion, diced
• 2 garlic cloves, chopped
• 2 celery stalks, chopped
• 2 cups brown lentils, rinsed
• 2 cups vegetable broth
• 4 cups kale, chopped
• 2 teaspoons smoked paprika
• 2 cups water
• Sea salt and black pepper, to taste

Instructions:
1. Heat olive oil in a large pot over medium-high heat.
2. Add carrots, onion, garlic, and celery and cook until vegetables are
softened and fragrant, about 5 minutes.
3. Add lentils, vegetable broth, kale, smoked paprika, and two cups of
water. Bring to a boil then reduce heat and simmer until lentils are
tender, about 25 minutes.
4. Season with salt and pepper to taste. Serve and enjoy.

Nutrition Information: (per serving)

Calories: 260 | Fat: 8g | Sodium: 370mg | Carbohydrates: 34g | Fiber: 10g | Protein: 16g

3. Greek Omelet with Feta and Olives

This Greek Omelet with Feta and Olives is a delicious, savory breakfast that comes together quickly. With healthy ingredients such as feta cheese and olives, this omelet is sure to please even the pickiest of eaters!
Serving: 2
| Preparation Time: 5 minutes
| Ready Time: 10 minutes

Ingredients:
- 4 large eggs
- 1/2 cup crumbled feta cheese
- 6 kalamata olives, pitted and chopped
- 2 tablespoons olive oil
- 1/4 teaspoon black pepper
- 1/4 teaspoon dried oregano

Instructions:
1. Whisk eggs in a bowl until combined.
2. Heat olive oil in a skillet over medium heat.
3. Pour egg mixture into the skillet.
4. Sprinkle feta cheese, olives and black pepper over the eggs.
5. Sprinkle oregano and cook for approximately 4-5 minutes, until eggs are cooked and lightly browned.
6. Place onto a plate and enjoy.

Nutrition Information:
- Calories: 450
- Total Fat: 35 g
- Saturated Fat: 14 g
- Cholesterol: 470 mg
- Sodium: 900 mg
- Total Carbohydrate: 5 g
- Dietary Fiber: 1 g
- Protein: 28 g

4. Spicy Tofu and Broccoli Stir-fry

Spicy Tofu and Broccoli Stir-fry is a quick and flavorful medley of vegetables and protein combining protein rich tofu, broccoli, onions and a homemade sauce.

Serving: 4
| Preparation Time: 10 minutes
| Ready Time: 20 minutes

Ingredients:
-1batch of firm tofu
-1 head of broccoli
-1 onion
-2-3 cloves of garlic
-1 teaspoon of coconut or vegetable oil
-1 cup of vegetable broth
-1 tablespoon of brown sugar
-2 tablespoons of soy sauce
-2 tablespoons of chili garlic sauce
-1 teaspoon of cornstarch

Instructions:
1. Cut the tofu into cubes and set on a paper towel to absorb some of the moisture.
2. Chop the onion and mince the garlic.
3. Cut the broccoli into small florets.
4. Heat the oil in a large pan over medium heat.
5. Add the onion and garlic and cook until fragrant.
6. Add the tofu and cook until slightly browned.
7. Add the broccoli and cook until just tender.
8. In a small bowl, whisk together the vegetable broth, brown sugar, soy sauce, chili garlic sauce, and cornstarch until combined.
9. Pour the sauce over the tofu and veggies and stir to coat.
10. Cook until the sauce is thick and bubbly.
11. Serve and enjoy!

Nutrition Information:

Calories: 175; Fat: 6.5g; Carbs: 15g; Protein: 10g

5. Avocado and Hummus Toast

This Avocado and Hummus Toast is a great, healthy and flavorful breakfast or snack that is easy to make. Servings: 1
| Preparation Time: 10 minutes
| Ready Time: 10 minutes

Ingredients:
-1 slice of toasted bread
-1 ripe avocado
-1 tablespoon of hummus
-Salt and pepper to taste

Instructions:
1. Toast bread slice
2. Slice avocado and spread it onto toast
3. Top the avocado with hummus
4. Add salt and pepper

Nutrition Information:
Calories: 290, Fat: 19 g, Protein: 5 g, Carbohydrates: 24 g, Sodium: 150 mg

6. Egg and Spinach Wrap

This easy-to-make Egg and Spinach Wrap is a delicious, healthy and convenient meal for busy days! It's family-friendly and perfect for an on-the-go breakfast or lunch.
Servings: 1
| Preparation Time: 5 minutes
| Ready Time: 15 minutes

Ingredients:
- 2 eggs
- 2 tablespoons skimmed milk

- Handful of baby spinach leaves
- 2 tablespoons grated cheddar cheese
- 1/2 teaspoon olive oil
- 10" (25 cm) whole wheat tortilla wrap

Instructions:
1. In a bowl, whisk together the eggs and the milk.
2. Heat the olive oil in a frying pan over medium heat.
3. Add the egg mixture and gently stir to keep it moving while it cooks.
4. When the eggs are nearly scrambled and still slightly wet, add the spinach leaves and stir until all the ingredients are evenly distributed.
5. Sprinkle the cheese, then turn off the heat and gently mix.
6. Transfer the filling to the wrap, fold the sides in and roll up into a wrap.

Nutrition Information:
Calories: 344
Fat: 16g
Carbohydrates: 29g
Protein: 17g

7. Turkey and Sweet Potato Quinoa Bowl

Turkey and Sweet Potato Quinoa Bowl is a delicious, clean-eating meal that's full of protein, fiber and other essential vitamins and minerals. This hearty and flavorful bowl is perfect for any time of year, and makes a great lunch or dinner.
Serving:4
| Preparation Time: 10 minutes
| Ready Time: 30 minutes

Ingredients:
-1 tablespoon olive oil
-1 small onion, diced
-1 lb ground turkey
-1/2 teaspoon ground cumin
-1/2 teaspoon smoked paprika
-2 cups cooked quinoa

-1 large sweet potato, peeled and diced
-1/2 teaspoon salt
-2 tablespoons lime juice
-1/4 cup chopped cilantro
-1/4 cup sliced almonds

Instructions:
1. Heat the olive oil in a large skillet over medium-high heat.
2. Add the onion and turkey, and cook until the turkey is lightly browned.
3. Add the cumin, paprika and sweet potato. Cook for 5 minutes.
4. Add the quinoa and salt and cook for another 5 minutes.
5. Add the lime juice and cilantro, and stir to combine.
6. Serve the turkey and sweet potato quinoa bowl topped with almonds.

Nutrition Information:
279 Calories, 28g Protein, 22g Carbs, 10g Fat, 5g Fiber.

8. Greek Yogurt and Overnight Oats

Greek Yogurt and Overnight Oats is a perfect healthy breakfast that can be easily prepared and sure to provide your body with a hit of protein and keep you full until lunch.
Serves 4. | Preparation Time: 5 minutes. | Ready Time: 8 hours.

Ingredients:
1. 1 cup rolled oats
2. 1 cup plain Greek yogurt
3. 1 cup almond milk
4. 2 tablespoons honey
5. 1 teaspoon cinnamon
6. 1/3 cup raisins

Instructions:
1. In a medium bowl, stir together the rolled oats, Greek yogurt, almond milk, honey and cinnamon.
2. Cover the bowl and let sit in the refrigerator for at least 8 hours or overnight.

3. In the morning, stir in the raisins and serve.

Nutrition Information:
Calories: 236 kcal, Carbohydrates: 39 g, Protein: 9 g, Fat: 5 g, Saturated Fat: 1 g, Sodium: 37 mg, Potassium: 211 mg, Fiber: 4 g, Sugar: 16 g, Vitamin A: 16 IU, Vitamin C: 0.2 mg, Calcium: 110 mg, Iron: 2 mg.

9. Grilled Chicken Caesar Salad

This delicious version of the classic Caesar salad includes grilled chicken for extra flavor and protein. A great way to enjoy a light meal, the Grilled Chicken Caesar Salad can be served as a main dish or side.
Serving: 4
| Preparation Time: 20 minutes
| Ready Time: 40 minutes

Ingredients:
• 2 boneless, skinless chicken breasts
• 2 tablespoons olive oil for marinating
• 2 heads romaine lettuce, chopped
• 2 tablespoons olive oil for dressing
• 4 tablespoons prepared Caesar dressing
• 2 tablespoons grated Parmesan cheese
• 2 tablespoons croutons

Instructions:
1. Preheat grill to medium heat.
2. Place chicken on plate and cover with 2 tablespoons of olive oil. Turn and coat both sides, ensuring all chicken is covered.
3. Place chicken on a greased grill, turning every 5 minutes until done.
4. In a large bowl, toss together lettuce and 2 tablespoons olive oil.
5. When chicken is done, remove from grill. Let cool before slicing into strips, set aside.
6. To assemble the salad, top the lettuce with the chicken strips, croutons, and dressing. Sprinkle with Parmesan cheese and toss all ingredients together.

Nutrition Information:

Per serving (4 servings): 300 calories; 21 g fat; 6 g carbohydrates; 16 g protein.

10. Baked Tuna and Vegetable Patties

This delicious and healthy Baked Tuna and Vegetable Patties recipe is a great combination of flavors! The patties are made with tuna, carrots, celery, cheese and other seasonings, and then baked until golden. The patties are perfect on top of sandwiches or as a vegetable side dish.
Serving: 4
| Preparation Time: 10 minutes

Ingredients:
- 2 cans of tuna, drained and flaked
- 1 carrot, finely chopped
- 1 stalk of celery, finely chopped
- 1/4 cup grated Parmesan cheese
- 1/4 cup Italian-style seasoned breadcrumbs
- 2 tablespoons fresh parsley, finely chopped
- 1 clove garlic, minced
- 1 egg, lightly beaten
- 1/4 teaspoon ground black pepper
- Cooking spray

Instructions:
1. Preheat oven to 350 degrees F (175 degrees C).
2. In a large bowl, mix together drained and flaked tuna, chopped carrot, chopped celery, Parmesan cheese, bread crumbs, parsley, garlic, egg, and pepper.
3. Shape the mixture into small patties and place on a baking sheet lined with parchment paper.
4. Spray each patty lightly with cooking spray.
5. Bake in preheated oven for 15 to 20 minutes, or until golden brown.

Nutrition Information:
Calories: 91
Total Fat: 3g
Saturated Fat: 1g

Cholesterol: 40mg
Sodium: 300mg
Total Carbohydrate: 6g
Protein: 10g

11. Eggplant and Lentil Curry

Eggplant and Lentil Curry is a spicy and flavorful vegan dish that's easy to make and full of protein. This tasty dish is perfect for a weeknight dinner or as a side dish to accompany other meals.
Serving: 4
| Preparation Time: 10 minutes
| Ready Time: 45 minutes

Ingredients:
1. 1/2 cup red lentils
2. 1 tablespoons olive oil
3. 1 large eggplant, diced
4. 1 onion, diced
5. 1 tablespoon minced ginger
6. 2 cloves garlic, minced
7. 1 teaspoon coriander
8. 1/2 teaspoon ground cumin
9. 1/4 teaspoon turmeric
10. 1 teaspoon sea salt
11. 3 cups water
12. 2 tablespoons lemon juice
13. 1 tablespoon cilantro, chopped

Instructions:
1. Place the lentils in a medium bowl and cover with hot water. Let sit for 10 minutes.
2. Heat the oil in a large saucepan on medium-high heat. Add the eggplant and onion and cook, stirring occasionally, for 10 minutes or until lightly browned.
3. Add the ginger, garlic, coriander, cumin, turmeric and sea salt and cook for 3 minutes, stirring often.

4. Add the water, lentils and lemon juice and bring to a boil. Reduce heat to medium and simmer, uncovered, for 30 minutes, stirring occasionally.
5. Add the cilantro and stir. Cook for an additional 5 minutes.
6. Serve and enjoy!

Nutrition Information:
Serving size: 1 cup
Calories: 170
Total Fat: 5 g
Saturated Fat: 1 g
Sodium: 400 mg
Total Carbohydrates: 24 g
Fiber: 3 g
Protein: 6 g

12. Seared Salmon with Asparagus

Seared Salmon with Asparagus is a delicious and fresh seafood dish that is easy to make and packed full of flavor.
Serving size: 4 | Preparation Time: 10 minutes | Ready Time: 30 minutes

Ingredients:
- 4 (5 ounces) Salmon fillets
- 2 tablespoons olive oil
- 2 tablespoons fresh lemon juice
- Salt and pepper to taste
- 2 tablespoons minced garlic
- 1 tablespoon chopped fresh parsley
- 1 pound fresh asparagus
- 2 tablespoons butter

Instructions:
1. Preheat oven to 400 degrees F (200 degrees C).
2. In a bowl, combine olive oil, lemon juice, salt, pepper, garlic and parsley. Mix together thoroughly.
3. Place salmon fillets on a lightly greased baking sheet. Brush the mixture evenly over each piece of salmon.

4. Place baking sheet in preheated oven and cook for 16-18 minutes or until salmon is cooked through.

5. In a separate skillet, melt butter over medium heat. Add in asparagus and cook for about 8 minutes or until asparagus is tender.

6. Plate the salmon, asparagus and serve.

Nutrition Information:
Calories: 310
Total fat: 17g
Cholesterol: 75mg
Sodium: 295mg
Total carbohydrates: 7.5g
Protein: 29g

13. Quinoa Taco Bowls

This delicious, vegetarian quinoa taco bowl is a perfect and healthy meal for lunch or dinner. It is full of plant-based proteins, fiber, and essential vitamins and minerals that your body needs.

Serving: 4
| Preparation Time: 15 minutes
| Ready Time: 15 minutes

Ingredients:
- 1 cup quinoa
- 1 can black beans, drained
- 2 cups cherry tomatoes (halved)
- 1 bell pepper (chopped)
- 1 red onion (diced)
- 1 avocado (diced)
- 2 tablespoons olive oil
- 1 tablespoon cumin
- 1 tablespoon chili powder
- Juice of 1 lime
- Salt and pepper to taste

Instructions:
1. Cook quinoa according to package instructions

2. In a large bowl, combine black beans, tomatoes, bell pepper, and onion
3. In a small bowl, whisk together olive oil, cumin, chili powder, lime juice, salt, and pepper
4. Pour the dressing over the salad mixture and stir together
5. Fluff the cooked quinoa and combine with the salad
6. Serve in individual bowls, top with diced avocado

Nutrition Information:
Calories: 294 kcal, Carbohydrates: 35g, Protein: 8g, Fat: 14g, Saturated Fat: 2g, Sodium: 52mg, Potassium: 643mg, Fiber: 9g, Sugar: 3g, Vitamin A: 655 IU, Vitamin C: 50.1mg, Calcium: 51mg, Iron: 2.2mg

14. Tempeh and Veggie Chili

Tempeh and Veggie Chili is a hearty vegetarian dish that is packed with flavor and nutrition. With a unique combination of protein-rich tempeh, beans, and flavorful vegetables, it makes the perfect comforting meal.
Serving: 4-6
| Preparation Time: 30 minutes
| Ready Time: 45 minutes

Ingredients:
1. 1 - 8 oz. package of tempeh, crumbled
2. 1 tablespoon olive oil
3. 1 onion, diced
4. 1 green bell pepper, diced
5. 1 jalapeno pepper, diced
6. 2 cloves garlic, minced
7. 1 teaspoon chili powder
8. 1 teaspoon cumin
9. 2 tablespoons tomato paste
10. 1 - 15oz can black beans, rinsed and drained
11. 1 - 15oz can pinto beans, rinsed and drained
12. 1 - 14.5oz can diced tomatoes
13. 1/2 cup vegetable broth
14. Salt and pepper to taste

Instructions:
1. Heat oil in a large skillet over medium heat. Add the crumbled tempeh, onion, bell pepper, jalapeno pepper, and garlic. Cook for 4-5 minutes, or until vegetables are softened.
2. Add chili powder, cumin, and tomato paste, and mix well. Cook for 2-3 minutes, or until fragrant.
3. Add black beans, pinto beans, diced tomatoes, vegetable broth, and salt and pepper. Stir until everything is combined. Simmer for 30 minutes, or until chili has thickened.

Nutrition Information:
Calories: 343, Fat: 6, Cholesterol: 0, Sodium: 511, Carbohydrates: 52, Protein: 20

15. Cauliflower Rice Burrito Bowl

Cauliflower Rice Burrito Bowl is a quick and flavorful vegan-friendly meal with a delicious blend of spices, veggies, and healthy grains. This burrito bowl is filling and easy to make.
Serving: 4
| Preparation Time: 15 minutes
| Ready Time: 30 minutes

Ingredients:
- 3 cups of cauliflower, riced
- 2 cups cooked brown rice
- 1/2 cup of black beans
- 1/2 cup corn
- 2 Roma tomatoes, diced
- 1/4 cup of sliced red onions
- 1/4 cup of diced jalapeno peppers
- 2 cloves of garlic, minced
- 1/2 teaspoon of chili powder
- 1/2 teaspoon of cumin
- 2 tablespoons olive oil
- Salt and pepper to taste

Instructions:

1. Preheat the oven to 400F.
2. Place the riced cauliflower onto a large baking sheet and spread it out in an even layer.
3. Drizzle the cauliflower with the olive oil, chili powder, cumin, salt and pepper, and toss well to combine.
4. Roast for 8 minutes.
5. Meanwhile, in a large skillet over medium heat, add the black beans, corn, tomatoes, red onions, and jalapeno peppers.
6. Saute for 8 minutes until the vegetables are cooked through.
7. Add the garlic and sauté for an additional 1-2 minutes.
8. Add the cooked brown rice and toss well to combine.
9. Remove the cauliflower from the oven and add it to the skillet.
10. Toss the burrito bowl until all of the ingredients are combined and heated through.
11. Serve warm.

Nutrition Information:
Calories: 192, Protein: 4.7 grams, Total Fat: 7.7 grams, Carbs: 27.7 grams, Fiber: 5.4 grams

16. Black Bean and Corn Salad

This vibrant and healthy black bean and corn salad is loaded with fresh ingredients and full of flavor. It is a perfect side dish for a cookout or summer picnic—or can be enjoyed as a light lunch!
Serving: Serves 8
| Preparation Time: 10 minutes
| Ready Time: 10 minutes

Ingredients:
- 1 (15-ounce) can black beans, rinsed and drained
- 1 (15-ounce) can corn, drained
- 1 bell pepper, diced
- 1/2 cup diced red onion
- 2 jalapeno peppers, seeded and diced
- 2 cloves garlic, minced
- 1/4 cup fresh cilantro, chopped
- 1/3 cup olive oil

- 2 tablespoons lime juice
- Salt and pepper to taste

Instructions:
1. In a large bowl, combine black beans, corn, bell pepper, red onion, jalapeno peppers, garlic, and cilantro.
2. In a small bowl, whisk together olive oil, lime juice, salt, and pepper.
3. Pour dressing over the salad ingredients and stir to combine.
4. Refrigerate for 30 minutes before serving.

Nutrition Information (per serving):
Calories: 150, Fat: 8 g, Cholesterol: 0 mg, Sodium: 125 mg, Carbohydrate: 18 g, Fiber: 4 g, Protein: 4 g

17. Grilled Beef Skewers with Chimichurri

Grilled Beef Skewers with Chimichurri are an easy and flavorful meal guaranteed to be a hit at any summer cookout. The perfect balance of savory and tangy flavors, this dish is sure to be a crowd-pleaser. With ingredients easy to find at any grocery store and a prep time of only fifteen minutes, this is an ideal dish to make on a busy weeknight.
Serving: 4
| Preparation Time: 15 minutes
| Ready Time: 20 minutes

Ingredients:
-1 lb flank steak
-2 tablespoons olive oil
-1/4 teaspoon black pepper
-1/4 teaspoon garlic powder
-1/2 cup parsley, chopped
-2 tablespoons oregano, chopped
-3 cloves garlic, minced
-salt, to taste
-1/4 cup red wine vinegar
-1/4 cup olive oil

Instructions:

1. Preheat the grill to medium-high heat.
2. Cut the flank steak into 1/2-inch cubes and season with the olive oil, garlic powder, and black pepper.
3. Thread the cubes onto skewers and place onto the preheated grill. Grill for about 7-8 minutes, flipping halfway through.
4. While the steak is grilling, combine the parsley, oregano, garlic, salt, red wine vinegar, and olive oil in a bowl to make a chimichurri sauce.
5. Once the steak is done grilling, remove from the heat and let rest for a few minutes. Serve the skewers with the chimichurri sauce.

Nutrition Information:
Calories: 412; Fat: 18g; Carbohydrates: 4g; Protein: 45g; Sodium: 25mg

18. Chicken and Spinach Stuffed Sweet Potato

This delicious Chicken and Spinach Stuffed Sweet Potato is a nutritious and flavorful meal that can be enjoyed at any time of the day. With its blend of protein, fiber and complex carbohydrates, it's also a great option for a satisfying lunch or dinner.
Serving: 4
| Preparation Time: 20 minutes
| Ready Time: 40 minutes

Ingredients:
-4 sweet potatoes
-1 tsp olive oil
-2 cups cooked chicken
-2 cups baby spinach
-1/4 cup diced red onion
-1 tsp garlic powder
-Salt and pepper to taste
-1/4 cup crumbled feta

Instructions:
1. Preheat oven to 400F. Pierce the sweet potatoes a few times with a fork and place onto a lined baking sheet. Bake in oven for 30-40 minutes or until tender.

2. Heat olive oil in a large skillet over medium-high heat. Add the cooked chicken, spinach, red onion, garlic powder, salt and pepper. Cook for about 5 minutes, or until lightly browned.

3. Cut the cooked sweet potatoes in half and scoop out some of the flesh from the center, leaving about 1/2" thickness.

4. Spoon the chicken and spinach mixture into the center of each sweet potato half and top with crumbled feta cheese. Place back into the oven and bake for an additional 8-10 minutes.

Nutrition Information:
One serving of Chicken and Spinach Stuffed Sweet Potato provides 370 calories, 10g fat, 35g carbohydrates, 33g protein, 5g fiber and 690mg sodium.

19. Halibut and Avocado Salad

A delicious Halibut and Avocado Salad, this is the perfect light meal for warm days.
Serving: 4
| Preparation Time: 10 minutes
| Ready Time: 15 minutes

Ingredients:
- 4 halibut filets
- 2 ripe avocados, sliced thinly
- 2 tablespoons of extra-virgin olive oil
- 1/4 cup lemon juice
- 2 tablespoons fresh chopped dill
- Salt and pepper, to taste

Instructions:
1. Preheat oven to 350 degrees.
2. Lightly oil a baking sheet and place halibut filets on sheet.
3. Bake for 10 minutes, or until filets are cooked through.
4. In a small bowl, whisk together olive oil, lemon juice, dill, salt and pepper.
5. Place halibut filets onto a salad plate and top with sliced avocados.
6. Drizzle with olive oil-lemon juice mixture.

Nutrition Information (per serving):
Calories: 190
Fat: 11 grams
Carbs: 4 grams
Protein: 15 grams

20. Turkey and Cheese Quesadillas

Turkey and Cheese Quesadillas are a delicious and easy-to-make meal that is perfect for lunch or dinner. With protein-packed turkey, melty cheese, and flavorful spices, this classic Tex-Mex dish is sure to become a favorite.
Serving: 4
| Preparation Time: 10 minutes

Ingredients:
- 2 tablespoons of olive oil
- 4 flour or corn tortillas
- 1 cup of cooked and cubed turkey
- 2 cups of shredded cheese, such as cheddar
- 1 cup of diced red onion
- 2 tablespoons of chopped cilantro
- 2 tablespoons of chili powder
- 1 teaspoon of garlic powder
- Salt and pepper, to taste

Instructions:
1. Heat the olive oil in a large skillet over medium heat.
2. Once the oil is hot, add one of the tortillas to the skillet and spread it with a spatula.
3. Add the cubed turkey, shredded cheese, diced red onion, cilantro, chili powder, garlic powder, and salt and pepper.
4. Place the second tortilla on top of the ingredients and press down gently to help the ingredients stick
5. Cook for 4-5 minutes, until the bottom tortilla is golden brown. Flip the quesadilla and cook for another 4-5 minutes.
6. Remove the quesadilla from the skillet, cut into four pieces, and serve.

7. Repeat with the remaining tortillas and ingredients.

Nutrition Information:
Calories: 416 kcal, Carbohydrates: 24g, Protein: 27g, Fat: 24g, Saturated
Fat: 13g, Cholesterol: 68mg, Sodium: 721mg, Potassium: 282mg, Fiber:
3g, Sugar: 2g, Vitamin A: 1230IU, Vitamin C: 3mg, Calcium: 351mg,
Iron: 2mg

21. Tofu and Spinach Stir-fry

Tofu and Spinach Stir-fry is an easy and delicious vegetarian dish. A
combination of savory tofu, nutrient-dense spinach, and earthy
mushrooms, this stir-fry is the perfect meal to satisfy all your nutritional
needs.
Serving: 4-6
Prep Time: 10 minutes
| Ready Time: 15 minutes

Ingredients:
• 3 cups fresh spinach
• 1/2 cup mushrooms, chopped
• 4 tablespoons vegetable oil
• 1 cup firm tofu, cubed
• 1 tablespoon soy sauce
• 2 tablespoons garlic, minced
• 1/2 teaspoon ground ginger

Instructions:
1. Heat 2 tablespoons of vegetable oil in a large skillet over medium-high
heat.
2. Once hot, add the tofu and cook until browned on all sides, about 5
minutes.
3. Remove the tofu from the skillet and set aside.
4. In the same skillet, heat the remaining 2 tablespoons of vegetable oil
over medium heat.
5. Add the mushrooms and garlic and cook until they become fragrant
and begin to brown, about 3 minutes.
6. Add the tofu, spinach, soy sauce, and ginger.

7. Cook until the spinach has wilted, about 2 minutes.
8. Serve hot.

Nutrition Information (per serving):
• Calories: 149
• Total Fat: 12g
• Cholesterol: 0mg
• Sodium: 176mg
• Carbohydrates: 5g
• Dietary Fiber: 2g
• Sugars: 1g
• Protein: 6g

22. Spicy Salmon Rice Bowl

This delicious and easy-to-make recipe for Spicy Salmon Rice Bowl is an excellent way to enjoy a healthy and fulfilling meal.
Serving: Serves two people.
| Preparation Time: 15 minutes
| Ready Time: 30 minutes

Ingredients:
- 2 Salmon fillets, 6oz each
- 2 cups cooked rice
- 2 tablespoons vegetable oil
- 1 teaspoon chilli flakes, or to taste
- 1 garlic clove, minced
- 1 teaspoon salt
- 1/4 cup soy sauce
- 1/4 cup mirin

Instructions:
1. Heat oil in a skillet over medium heat.
2. Place the salmon fillets in the skillet and season with chilli flakes, garlic, salt and soy sauce.
3. Cook on each side for 4-6 minutes, or until cooked through.
4. Transfer the cooked salmon to a plate.
5. In the same skillet, add the cooked rice and heat for 1-2 minutes.

6. Pour in the mirin and season with soy sauce and salt to taste.

7. Stir to combine.

8. Serve half of the cooked salmon and half of the cooked rice in each bowl.

Nutrition Information:
Per Serving - Calories: 586, Fat: 28.3g, Carbohydrates: 36.2g, Protein: 36.5g.

23. Baked Tofu Nuggets

Baked Tofu Nuggets are a great vegan, healthy alternative to fried chicken nuggets. These delicious baked nuggets are made with crispy, sprouted tofu and herbs, which provide amazing flavor.
Serving: 4
| Preparation Time: 15 minutes
| Ready Time: 40 minutes

Ingredients:
-1 block extra-firm sprouted tofu
-1/2 cup almond meal
-2 teaspoons garlic powder
-1 teaspoon dried thyme
-1/2 teaspoon sea salt
-1/4 teaspoon black pepper
-1/4 teaspoon smoked paprika
-2 tablespoons olive oil

Instructions:
1. Preheat the oven to 400F (200C).
2. Place the tofu on a cutting board and press it with a kitchen towel and something heavy for about five minutes, to remove excess moisture.
3. Cut the pressed tofu into 1/2 inch cubes.
4. In a medium-sized bowl, mix together the almond meal, garlic powder, thyme, sea salt, black pepper and smoked paprika.
5. Drizzle the tofu cubes with the olive oil and toss to coat.
6. Add the tofu cubes to the bowl with the almond meal mixture and stir to coat the tofu cubes.

7. Line a baking sheet with parchment paper and place the tofu cubes on the baking sheet.
8. Bake for 20-30 minutes, or until the nuggets are golden brown and crispy.
9. Remove from the oven and allow the nuggets to cool for 5 minutes before serving.

Nutrition Information:
Per serving:
Calories: 206, Fat: 12g, Carbohydrates: 8g, Protein: 16g, Fiber: 3g, Sodium: 286mg

24. Lentil and Egg Salad

Gaining countless applause among health conscious individuals, this protein packed Lentil and Egg Salad is a perfect way to include more fiber in your diet.
Serve 4; | Preparation Time 15 minutes; Ready in 15 minutes.

Ingredients:
- 1 cup dry lentils
- 2 cups of water
- 2 boiled eggs
- 1 diced red onion
- 1 diced cucumber
- 2 tablespoons of mayonnaise
- 1 teaspoon of ground mustard
- 1 teaspoon of lime juice
- Salt and pepper to taste

Instructions:
1. In a saucepan, bring water and lentils to a boil.
2. Reduce heat and simmer for 10-15 minutes until lentils are cooked but still firm.
3. While lentils are cooking, hard boil two eggs and dice both the onion and cucumber.
4. Drain the cooked lentils and rinse under cold water.

5. In a large bowl, combine cooked lentils, diced onion, cucumber and eggs.
6. Add mayonnaise, ground mustard and lime juice.
7. Gently stir to mix the ingredients together.
8. Add salt and pepper to taste.

Nutrition Information:
Calories: 272
Fat: 9g
Carbs: 32g
Protein: 14g

25. Peanut Butter and Banana Overnight Oats

Peanut Butter and Banana Overnight Oats is a delicious and healthy breakfast, perfect for busy mornings! It combines the flavors of banana, peanuts, and oats for a flavorful, hearty breakfast.
Serving: 1, | Preparation Time: 5 minutes, | Ready Time: overnight,

Ingredients:
-1/2 banana, mashed
-1/4 cup rolled oats
-1/4 cup almond or coconut milk
-1 tablespoon natural peanut butter
-1 teaspoon honey (optional)

Instructions:
1. In a bowl, mash the banana until it is smooth.
2. Add the oats, almond or coconut milk, peanut butter, and honey (if using) to the bowl.
3. Mix all ingredients well.
4. Cover the bowl and place in refrigerator overnight.
5. In the morning, enjoy your overnight oats cold or warmed up.

Nutrition Information:
-Calories: 236
-Fat: 11.5g
-Carbohydrates: 28g

-Protein: 7.2g

26. Kidney Bean and Quinoa Stew

This delicious, hearty, and protein rich vegan stew combines two of the best superfoods - quinoa and kidney beans. It's easy to make and perfect for meal prepping.
Serving: Serves 4
| Preparation Time: 5 minutes
| Ready Time: 20 minutes

Ingredients:
-1.5 cups of cooked quinoa
-1.5 cups of cooked kidney beans
-1/2 a white onion, diced
-1 red bell pepper, diced
-4 cloves of garlic, minced
-1 large tomato, diced
-2 tablespoons of olive oil
-2 cups of vegetable broth
-1 teaspoon of cumin
-1 teaspoon of smoked paprika
-1 teaspoon of oregano
-Salt and pepper, to taste

Instructions:
1. Heat olive oil in a large pot over medium-high heat.
2. Add onion and red pepper and sauté for 3-4 minutes, until softened.
3. Add garlic and sauté for another 1 minute.
4. Add tomato, cumin, smoked paprika, oregano, and vegetable broth. Bring to a boil, then reduce heat and simmer for 10 minutes.
5. Add cooked quinoa, kidney beans, and salt and pepper. Simmer for an additional 5 minutes.
6. Serve with additional garnishes, if desired.

Nutrition Information:
Calories: 272; Fat: 8.5g; Carbs: 35g; Protein: 15g

27. Turkey Burger with Avocado

This Turkey Burger with Avocado is a delicious, healthy and easy-to-make meal. All you need are some simple ingredients, including ground turkey and fresh avocado. A great option for a quick lunch or dinner, this turkey burger recipe is versatile and filling.

Serving: 4
| Preparation Time: 10 minutes
| Ready Time: 25 minutes

Ingredients:
- 1 lb ground turkey
- 1 tablespoon olive oil
- 1/2 teaspoon garlic powder
- 1/2 teaspoon onion powder
- 1 teaspoon of smoked paprika
- 1/4 teaspoon of black pepper
- 1/4 teaspoon of kosher salt
- 4 hamburger buns
- 1/2 avocado, sliced

Instructions:
1. Preheat oven to 350F.
2. In a large bowl, mix together the ground turkey, olive oil, garlic powder, onion powder, smoked paprika, black pepper and kosher salt.
3. Form the turkey into four 1/2 inch thick patties and place them on a baking sheet.
4. Bake for 15 minutes, and then carefully turn the burgers over and bake for an additional 10 minutes.
5. Toast the hamburger buns while turkey burgers are baking.
6. Serve the turkey burgers on the hamburger buns with avocado slices.

Nutrition Information:
Calories: 439, Fat: 17g, Saturated Fat: 4g, Sodium 487mg, Carbohydrates: 32g, Fiber: 4g, Protein: 33g.

28. Black Bean and Avocado Burrito

With a flavour combination of creamy avocado and earthy black beans, this black bean and avocado burrito is a delicious and healthy Mexican-inspired meal.
Serving: 8
| Preparation Time: 15 minutes
| Ready Time: 45 minutes

Ingredients:
- 2 cups cooked black beans
- 2 avocados, cubed
- 1/2 cup onion, chopped
- 2 cloves garlic, minced
- 2 tablespoons olive oil
- 2 tablespoons lime juice
- 1 teaspoon chili powder
- 1 teaspoon ground cumin
- 8 flour tortillas

Instructions:
1. Heat the olive oil in a large skillet over medium-high heat.
2. Add the onion and garlic, and sauté for 5 minutes.
3. Add the black beans, chili powder, and cumin and cook for an additional 5 minutes.
4. Remove from heat and stir in the lime juice and avocado.
5. Divide the mixture among the 8 tortillas and wrap each one like a burrito.
6. Place the burritos on a baking sheet and bake in a preheated oven at 375F (190°C) for 30 minutes.

Nutrition Information:
Calories: 240; Total Fat: 9g; Saturated Fat: 1g; Cholesterol: 0mg; Sodium: 200mg; Total Carbohydrate: 39g; Dietary Fiber: 10g; Protein: 8g

29. Grilled Salmon with Spinach

This dish is the perfect combination of healthy and delicious – Grilled Salmon with Spinach. The subtle sweetness of salmon pairs wonderfully with the earthy taste of spinach and is easy to prepare, with a healthy dose of vitamins and minerals.

Serving: Makes 4 servings
| Preparation Time: 10 minutes
| Ready Time: 15 minutes

Ingredients:
- 4 (6 ounce) salmon fillets
- 2 tablespoons olive oil
- Salt and black pepper to taste
- 2 cups fresh spinach leaves
- 2 tablespoons reduced-fat butter

Instructions:
1. Preheat a grill pan over medium-high heat.
2. Brush the salmon fillets with olive oil and season with salt and pepper.
3. Grill the salmon for 5 minutes. Flip, and then top each fillet with a handful of spinach leaves and a slice of butter.
4. Grill for an additional 5 minutes, or until the flesh flakes easily with a fork and the spinach is wilted.

Nutrition Information:
Calories: 264 kcal, Carbohydrates: 0.8 g, Protein: 29.3 g, Fat: 16.2 g, Saturated Fat: 5.2 g, Cholesterol: 79 mg, Sodium: 122 mg, Potassium: 650 mg, Fiber: 0.6 g, Sugar: 0.1 g, Vitamin A: 1485 IU, Vitamin C: 3 mg, Calcium: 52 mg, Iron: 1 mg.

30. Chickpea and Kale Salad

This Mediterranean-inspired Chickpea and Kale Salad is a delicious, nutritious meal full of fresh vegetables, herbs, and healthy fats. The chickpeas and sunflower seeds add a hint of crunch, while the feta cheese adds a salty, creamy finish. It's an easy and flavorful meal that can be served as a side dish or even a main course.

Serving: 4-6
| Preparation Time: 15 minutes

| Ready Time: 15 minutes

Ingredients:
- 2 bunches kale, washed, dried and torn into pieces
- 2 cups cooked chickpeas
- 2 tablespoons olive oil
- 3 tablespoons lemon juice
- 2 cloves of garlic, minced
- 2 tablespoons fresh chopped flat-leaf parsley
- 1/3 cup sunflower seeds
- 2 tablespoons crumbled feta cheese
- Salt and pepper to taste

Instructions:
1. In a large mixing bowl, combine the kale and chickpeas.
2. In a small bowl, whisk together the olive oil, lemon juice, garlic, parsley, sunflower seeds, feta cheese, and salt and pepper.
3. Drizzle the dressing over the kale and chickpeas, and toss to combine.
4. Serve immediately, or store in the refrigerator for up to 3 days.

Nutrition Information:
Serving size: one serving
Calories: 187
Fat: 12g
Carbohydrates: 16g
Protein: 6g
Fiber: 5g

31. Greek Avocado Salad

This Greek Avocado Salad is a delicious, light lunch/dinner recipe that is easy to make and full of nutrition. This hearty, refreshing combination of feta, olives, tomatoes and avocado makes it a powerhouse of flavor, color, and crunch.
Serving: 4
| Preparation Time: 10 mins
Ready: 10 mins

Ingredients:
- 1 small red onion, diced
- 2 avocados, peeled, pitted and lightly cubed
- 2 cups cherry tomatoes, halved
- 1 cup crumbled feta cheese
- 2/3 cup crumbled black olives
- 2 tablespoons olive oil
- 2 tablespoons red wine vinegar
- 1 tablespoon chopped fresh oregano
- Salt and freshly ground black pepper, to taste

Instructions:
1. In a large bowl, combine the onion, avocado, tomatoes, feta, and olives.
2. In a small bowl, whisk together the olive oil, red wine vinegar, and oregano. Pour this over the salad and mix everything together.
3. Season with salt and pepper and serve.

Nutrition Information:
Calories: 290; Total Fat: 23g; Saturated Fat: 6g; Cholesterol: 25mg; Sodium: 470mg; Carbohydrates: 11g; Fiber: 6g; Protein: 7g.

32. Mediterranean Chickpea Salad

This Mediterranean Chickpea Salad is a delicious and healthy dish that is full of flavor! It's the perfect side dish or light meal, and it comes together in no time.
Serving: 6-8
| Preparation Time: 10 minutes
| Ready Time: 10 minutes

Ingredients:
- 2 cans (15-ounce) chickpeas, drained and rinsed
- 1 red bell pepper, diced
- 1/3 cup diced red onion
- 1/2 large cucumber, peeled and diced
- 1/4 cup chopped fresh parsley
- 2 cloves garlic, minced

- 2 tablespoons olive oil
- 1/4 cup fresh lemon juice
- 1 teaspoon dried oregano
- Salt and freshly ground black pepper, to taste

Instructions:
1. In a large bowl, combine chickpeas, bell pepper, red onion, cucumber, and parsley.
2. In a small bowl, whisk together garlic, olive oil, lemon juice and oregano. Season with salt and pepper, to taste.
3. Pour the dressing over the salad. Gently Toss to combine.

Nutrition Information:
Calories: 220, Total Fat: 10g, Saturated Fat: 1.5g, Cholesterol: 0mg, Sodium: 174mg, Carbohydrate: 27g, Dietary Fiber: 8g, Sugars: 2g, Protein: 10g.

33. Quinoa Crusted Chicken Fingers

Quinoa Crusted Chicken Fingers is a delicious, crunchy, and healthy alternative to traditional fried chicken finger recipes. The quinoa adds an unexpected crunch to the chicken and provides a boost of nutrition too. Serves 4, | Preparation Time 15 minutes, Ready in 20-25 minutes.

Ingredients:
•1/2 cup quinoa (uncooked)
•3 eggs
•3 tablespoons olive oil
•1 cup breadcrumbs
•1 cup grated Parmesan cheese
•1 teaspoon garlic powder
•1 teaspoon parsley flakes
•Salt and pepper, to taste
•1 pound chicken tenders

Instructions:
1. Preheat your oven to 425 degrees F.
2. Prepare the quinoa according to package instructions.

3. In a shallow bowl, mix together the eggs and olive oil.

4. In another bowl, combine the breadcrumbs, grated Parmesan cheese, garlic powder, parsley, salt, and pepper.

5. Dip the chicken tenders in the egg mixture and then coat with the crumb mixture. Place the coated chicken tenders on a lined baking sheet.

6. Bake for 15-20 minutes or until the chicken is cooked through and the coating is golden brown.

Nutrition Information:
Calories: 320, Total Fat: 13.2g, Saturated Fat: 3.9g, Cholesterol: 120mg, Sodium: 535mg, Carbohydrates: 16.4g, Fiber: 1.3g, Sugar: 1.3g, Protein: 30.4g.

34. Zucchini and Egg Frittata

This Zucchini and Egg Frittata is an easy, healthy and delicious breakfast, lunch, or even dinner option! This frittata is packed with protein and flavor from the zucchini, eggs and seasoning. Serve it up with a side of fruit or a small salad for an even more balanced meal.

Serving: 6
| Preparation Time: 10 minutes
| Ready Time: 35 minutes

Ingredients:
1.   3 tablespoons olive oil
2.   1 cup diced onion
3.   1 garlic clove, minced
4.   2 cups diced zucchini
5.   8 large eggs, lightly beaten
6.   3 tablespoons grated Parmesan cheese
7.   1 tablespoon chopped fresh oregano, or 1 teaspoon dried oregano
8.   1/2 teaspoon salt
9.   1/4 teaspoon black pepper

Instructions:
1. Preheat oven to 350 degrees F (175 degrees C).

2. Heat olive oil in a large skillet over medium heat. Cook onions in oil for 4 minutes, stirring occasionally. Stir in garlic and zucchini and cook 5 more minutes.

3. In a large bowl, whisk the eggs together with the Parmesan cheese, oregano, salt and pepper.

4. Pour the onion and zucchini mixture into the egg mixture and stir to combine until everything is evenly distributed.

5. Pour the mixture into a greased glass 9-inch pie plate.

6. Bake for 30 minutes, or until the center has set.

Nutrition Information: (per serving)
Calories: 140 kcal
Protein: 7 g
Carbohydrates: 3.5 g
Fiber: 1 g
Total Fat: 11 g
Saturated Fat: 2.7 g
Cholesterol: 186 mg
Sodium: 278 mg

35. Buffalo Chicken Wraps

Buffalo Chicken Wraps are a spicy twist on classic chicken wraps perfect for snacks or lunch. Featuring cooked chicken tossed in a spicy buffalo sauce and served on a wrap with fresh veggies, this wrap will tantalize your taste buds!
Serving: 4
| Preparation Time: 10 minutes
| Ready Time: 10 minutes

Ingredients:
- 4 large tortilla wraps
- 2 cooked chicken breasts, diced
- 2 tablespoons buffalo sauce
- 1/2 cup chopped celery
- 1/4 cup sliced red onions
- 1/4 cup shredded carrots
- 2 tablespoons ranch dressing

Instruction:

1. Spread each tortilla wrap on a flat surface.
2. In a bowl, combine chicken and buffalo sauce. Mix until combined.
3. Divide chicken and vegetables among the four wraps.
4. Drizzle ranch dressing over the wraps.
5. Roll the wraps up tightly.
6. Slice wraps in half diagonally and serve.

Nutrition Information:

Calories: 393 kcal, Carbohydrates: 25 g, Protein: 24 g, Fat: 21 g, Saturated Fat: 4.5 g, Cholesterol: 68 mg, Sodium: 824 mg, Potassium: 227 mg, Fiber: 2.5 g, Sugar: 1.5 g, Vitamin A: 1270 IU, Vitamin C: 3.2 mg, Calcium: 88 mg, Iron: 1.5 mg.

36. Taco Salad with Chicken

Taco Salad with Chicken is a hearty and flavorful meals perfect for dinner or lunch. It's packed with Mexican-inspired flavors like beef, beans and cheese, and topped with a delicious Catalina dressing.
Serving: 8
| Preparation Time: 20 minutes
| Ready Time: 8 hours

Ingredients:

- 1 lb. ground beef
- 1 pkg. taco seasoning
- 1 (30 oz) can red beans, rinsed and drained
- 1 (15 oz) can corn, drained
- 1 (16 oz) bottle Catalina dressing
- 1 cup cheddar cheese, shredded
- 2 cups salsa
- 1/2 cup black olives, chopped
- 1/3 cup green onions, chopped
- 1 head romaine lettuce, chopped
- 2 cups cooked chicken, diced

Instructions:

1. In a large skillet, cook ground beef until brown, breaking up with a spoon. Drain fat.
2. Add taco seasoning and stir, cooking for a few minutes.
3. In a large bowl, combine beans, corn, Catalina dressing, cheese, salsa, olives, green onions, and lettuce. Stir in cooked ground beef.
4. Cover and refrigerate for at least 8 hours.
5. Before serving, stir in chicken, and serve.

Nutrition Information:
Serving Size - 1 cup, Calories: 279, Total Fat: 8.7g, Saturated fat: 3.9g, Cholesterol: 39mg, Sodium: 566mg, Carbohydrates: 24.6g, Fiber: 7.3g, Protein: 22.9g

37. Veggie Omelet with Goat Cheese

This delicious and healthy Veggie Omelet with Goat Cheese is a great start to any day! Enjoy the combination of vegetables and creamy goat cheese, guaranteed to please your taste buds. It is a relatively simple dish to make and serves 4 people. It takes about 10 minutes to prepare and about 10 minutes to cook, adding up to a total ready time of 20 minutes.
Serving: 4
| Preparation Time: 10 minutes
| Ready Time: 20 minutes

Ingredients:
- 4 eggs
- 2 tsp butter
- 1/2 cup chopped mushrooms
- 1/2 cup diced peppers
- 1/2 cup diced onions
- 1/3 cup crumbled goat cheese
- Salt and pepper

Instructions:
1. Whip the eggs in a bowl and season with salt and pepper.
2. Heat the butter in an omelet pan over medium-high heat.
3. Add the vegetables to the pan and cook for 2-3 minutes, stirring occasionally.

4. Pour the egg mixture into the pan and stir to combine.

5. Sprinkle the crumbled goat cheese over the top of the omelet.

6. Fold the omelet in half and cook for 1-2 minutes until lightly browned.

7. Flip the omelet and cook for an additional 1-2 minutes.

8. Serve and enjoy!

Nutrition Information:
Calories: 188, Carbohydrates: 4g, Protein: 10g, Fat: 14g, Saturated Fat: 6g, Cholesterol: 180g, Sodium: 160mg, Fiber: 1g, Sugar: 2g

38. Grilled Tofu and Vegetables

Grilled Tofu and Vegetables is a healthy and delicious meal that can be served as a side dish or main course. Boasting with nutritional benefits, this dish is also easy to prepare and can be whipped up in less than 30 minutes.

Serving: 4-6
| Preparation Time: 10 minutes
| Ready Time: 15-20 minutes

Ingredients:
• 1 block extra firm tofu, cut into cubes
• 2 medium zucchinis, sliced into thin rounds
• 1 bell pepper, sliced into strips
• 1 red onion, sliced into thin wedges
• 1 teaspoon garlic powder
• 2 tablespoons olive oil
• Salt and pepper to taste

Instructions:
1. Preheat the grill to medium heat.
2. In a large bowl, mix together the tofu cubes, zucchini slices, bell pepper strips, red onion wedges, garlic powder, olive oil, salt and pepper.
3. Preheat the grill to medium heat.
4. Place the tofu and vegetable mixture onto a greased grill and cook for 15-20 minutes until the vegetables are tender, flipping the mixture halfway through cooking.

Nutrition Information:
Calories: 151 | Fat: 9 g | Sodium: 30 mg | Carbohydrates: 10 g | Fiber: 3 g | Protein: 9 g

39. Baked Tofu and Kale Bowl

This Baked Tofu and Kale Bowl is the perfect dinner - loaded with healthy, delicious ingredients and full of flavor. A simple combination of tofu, kale, tomatoes, and quinoa all baked to perfection, it's sure to satisfy the whole family!
Serving: 4
| Preparation Time: 10 minutes
| Ready Time: 35 minutes

Ingredients:
1. 1 package organic extra-firm tofu, drained and pressed
2. 2 tablespoons olive oil
3. 1 teaspoon garlic powder
4. 1 teaspoon smoked paprika
5. 1 teaspoon sea salt
6. 1/2 teaspoon black pepper
7. 1/2 cup uncooked quinoa
8. 1 cup vegetable broth
9. 1 cup chopped tomatoes
10. 2 cups kale, chopped
11. Optional: 2 tablespoons nutritional yeast

Instructions:
1. Preheat oven to 400F.
2. Line a baking sheet with parchment paper and spread out the tofu.
3. Drizzle the tofu with olive oil and sprinkle garlic powder, smoked paprika, sea salt, and black pepper on top.
4. Bake for 20 minutes, flipping the tofu halfway through.
5. Meanwhile, prepare quinoa according to package instructions in vegetable broth.
6. About 5 minutes before the tofu is ready, add chopped tomatoes and kale to the baking sheet around the tofu.

7. Bake for an additional 10 minutes, or until the kale is lightly browned and the tofu is crispy.

8. Serve the cooked quinoa with the tofu and vegetables.

9. Optional: sprinkle with nutritional yeast for a cheesy flavor.

Nutrition Information:
Per Serving (4 servings): Calories: 364, Fat: 18g, Carbohydrates: 32g, Fiber: 7g, Protein: 18g.

40. Curried Quinoa and Vegetables

Curried Quinoa and Vegetables is a healthy and flavorful dish that combines protein-packed quinoa with a variety of fresh vegetables cooked in a rich, aromatic curry sauce. This easy-to-make dish is perfect for a delicious and nutritious mid-week meal.

Serving: 4-6
| Preparation Time: 15 minutes
| Ready Time: 35 minutes

Ingredients:
- 1 cup quinoa, rinsed and drained
- 1 tablespoon olive oil
- 1 onion, diced
- 1 red bell pepper, diced
- 1 cup frozen peas
- 2 cloves garlic, minced
- 2 teaspoons curry powder
- 1 teaspoon turmeric
- 1/4 teaspoon cayenne pepper, optional
- 1 14-ounce can diced tomatoes
- 2 cups vegetable broth
- Salt and freshly ground black pepper, to taste

Instructions:
1. Heat the oil in a large saucepan over medium heat. Add the onion, bell pepper, and garlic and cook until softened, about 5 minutes.

2. Add the curry powder, turmeric, and cayenne and cook, stirring, for 1 minute.

3. Add the tomatoes, broth, and quinoa, and bring to a boil.

4. Reduce the heat to low, cover the pan and simmer until the quinoa is cooked through and the vegetables are tender, about 20 minutes.

5. Add the peas during the last 5 minutes of cooking.

6. Season with salt and pepper to taste.

7. Serve hot.

Nutrition Information: (per serving)
Calories: 235 | Fat: 4.9g | Saturated Fat: 0.7g | Carbohydrates: 38.2g | Sugar: 6.2g | Fiber: 6.9g | Protein: 9.1g

41. Egg and Tomato Breakfast Sandwich

This delicious Egg and Tomato Breakfast Sandwich is the perfect way to start your day with a nutritious and balanced breakfast.
Serving: 1 person
| Preparation Time: 10 minutes
| Ready Time: 10 minutes

Ingredients:
- 2 slices of whole wheat bread
- 2 eggs
- 2 slices of tomato
- Salt & pepper to taste
- 1 tablespoon of butter
- 1 teaspoon of olive oil

Instructions:
1. Heat the butter and olive oil in a medium-sized skillet over medium heat.
2. Crack the eggs into the skillet and season with salt and pepper.
3. Cook the eggs until they are cooked to your liking.
4. Toast the bread in a toaster or over a skillet.
5. Assemble the sandwich by layering the tomato and eggs between the two slices of toast.
6. Enjoy your Egg and Tomato Breakfast Sandwich.

Nutrition Information:

Calories: 253 kcal,
Carbohydrates: 20.2 g,
Protein: 14.2 g,
Fat: 13 g,
Saturated Fat: 5.2 g,
Cholesterol: 203 mg,
Sodium: 433 mg,
Fiber: 6.3 g.

42. Fried Rice with Edamame and Veggies

This delicious fried rice dish is a healthy and flavorful combination of edamame, fresh vegetables, and long grain rice paired with a hint of soy sauce.
Serving: 4-6
| Preparation Time: 25 minutes
| Ready Time: 55 minutes

Ingredients:
- 2 cups long grain rice
- 2 cups frozen edamame
- 2-3 tablespoons vegetable oil
- 2 cloves garlic, minced
- 2 stalks celery, diced
- 1 cup carrots, diced
- 1 small onion, diced
- 2 tablespoons soy sauce
- Salt and pepper to taste

Instruction:
1. Begin by cooking the long grain rice according to package instructions.
2. Meanwhile, heat 1 tablespoon of the vegetable oil in a large skillet over medium high heat.
3. Add in the edamame and cook for 3-4 minutes, stirring frequently.
4. Add the garlic, celery, carrots and onions to the skillet and cook for an additional 5-6 minutes, stirring frequently.
5. Push the vegetables to one side of the skillet and add in the remaining oil.

6. Add in the cooked rice and season with the soy sauce, salt and pepper. Mix everything together and cook for an additional 3-4 minutes.
7. Serve the fried rice with fresh vegetables and enjoy!

Nutrition Information (Per Serving):
Calories: 266, Fat: 5.8g, Carbs: 43.7g, Protein: 12.3g

43. Eggplant and Tofu lasagna

Eggplant and Tofu Lasagna is a delicious and vegan-friendly twist on a classic Italian dish. This recipe packs loads of flavor, providing a hearty, satisfying meal that can be enjoyed by both meat eaters and vegetarians alike.
Serving: 4-6
| Preparation Time: 20 minutes
| Ready Time: 45 minutes

Ingredients:
• 2 tablespoons olive oil
• 1 large eggplant, sliced into 1/2-inch thick pieces
• 1 onion, peeled and diced
• 4 cloves garlic, minced
• 1 (14-ounce) package firm tofu
• 1 (15-ounce) container ricotta cheese
• 1 (8-ounce) package shredded vegan Italian cheese
• 2 (14.5-ounce) cans diced tomatoes
• 2 teaspoons Italian seasoning
• Salt and freshly ground black pepper
• 1 (16-ounce) package lasagna noodles
• Chopped parsley, for garnish (optional)

Instructions:
1. Preheat oven to 375 degrees Fahrenheit.
2. Heat the olive oil in a large skillet over medium-high heat. Add the eggplant and cook, stirring occasionally, until tender, about 5 minutes. Add the onion and garlic and cook, stirring occasionally, until the vegetables are softened and lightly golden, about 5 minutes more.

3. In a small bowl, mash the tofu with a fork. Add to the skillet and cook, stirring occasionally, until lightly golden, about 5 minutes.

4. Spread a layer of ricotta cheese over the bottom of a 9 x 13 inch baking dish. Top with a layer of lasagna noodles, followed by a layer of the eggplant and tofu mixture, and a layer of diced tomatoes. Sprinkle with Italian seasoning and salt and pepper. Repeat layering until all ingredients are used.

5. Sprinkle with the shredded vegan cheese. Cover with foil and bake for 35 minutes.

6. Remove foil, turn the oven to broil and cook for an additional 5 minutes, or until lightly golden.

7. Garnish with chopped parsley, if desired, and serve.

Nutrition Information:
Calories: 294, Fat: 10g, Cholesterol: 0mg, Sodium: 185mg, Carbohydrates: 33g, Fiber: 4.9g, Protein: 11.7g

44. Lemon and Dill Salmon Salad

This Lemon and Dill Salmon Salad makes a delicious light and healthy meal. Serve it as an entree or as part of a main dish. It's a great way to enjoy healthy salmon and feel energized afterward.
Serving: 4
| Preparation Time: 10 minutes

Ingredients:
-4 boneless salmon fillets
-4 tablespoon lemon juice
-2 tablespoon olive oil
-2 tablespoons chopped fresh dill
-Salt and pepper to taste
-4 cups mixed greens
-1/4 cup slivered almonds
-1/4 cup feta cheese

Instructions:
1. Preheat oven to 400F

2. Place the salmon fillets in a baking dish, and season with lemon juice, olive oil, dill, salt and pepper.
3. Bake in preheated oven for 12-15 minutes, or until the salmon is cooked through.
4. In a large bowl, combine the mixed greens, almonds and feta cheese.
5. Place the cooked salmon fillets on top and drizzle with remaining lemon juice and olive oil mixture
6. Serve the salad with a crusty loaf, or with lemon wedges.

Nutrition Information:
Calories:374, Total Fat:18.3g, Saturated Fat:3.3g, Cholesterol:89.5mg, Sodium:155.6mg, Potassium:487 mg, Carbohydrates:8.5g, Dietary Fiber:2.5g, Sugars:1.9g, Protein:39.9g

45. Tuna Salad Lettuce Wraps

Tuna Salad Lettuce Wraps are a delicious and healthy way to enjoy a light lunch or dinner that is packed full of flavor. With fresh tuna, crisp vegetables, and salty feta cheese all wrapped in crisp lettuce, these wraps make for a satisfying meal in minutes.
Serves 4; | Preparation Time 10 minutes; ready in 10 minutes.

Ingredients:
- 2 cans of Albacore tuna in water, drained
- 1/2 red onion, diced
- 2 large tomatoes, diced
- 1 large cucumber, diced
- 4 ounces feta cheese, crumbled
- 2 tablespoons extra-virgin olive oil
- 1 teaspoon freshly ground black pepper
- 1/2 teaspoon garlic powder
- Salt and freshly ground black pepper, to taste
- 8 large lettuce leaves

Instructions:
1. In a large bowl, combine the tuna, red onion, diced tomatoes, cucumber, feta cheese, and olive oil.

2. Season with black pepper, garlic powder, and a pinch of salt and pepper.
3. Gently mix all ingredients together.
4. Divide the filling among the lettuce leaves. Then, fold the leaves over to create a wrap.

Nutrition Information (per serving):
Calories: 246; Fat: 12 g; Sodium: 559 mg; Carbohydrates: 11 g; Fiber: 2 g; Protein: 19 g

46. Turkey and Avocado Sandwich

Turkey and Avocado Sandwich is an easy yet flavorful sandwich that is sure to satisfy. This sandwich features creamy avocado, juicy turkey, and your favorite condiments, all toasted to perfection. Serve with a side of crunchy chips or your favorite salad for a complete meal.
Serving: 4
| Preparation Time: 5 minutes
| Ready Time: 10 minutes

Ingredients:
- 4 slices of whole wheat or sourdough bread
- 4-ounce cooked turkey sliced
- 1 large-sized avocado, seeded and sliced
- 2 tablespoons cream cheese
- 4 tablespoons of your favorite condiments like mayonnaise, mustard, ranch, etc
- Lettuce leaves of your choice

Instructions:
1. Toast each slice of bread until golden brown and lightly crisp.
2. Spread cream cheese over each slice of toasted bread.
3. Add condiments to two slices of the toast.
4. On top of the condiment-topped slices of toast, layer one of the non-condiment-topped slices followed by a layer of turkey, avocado, and lettuce leaves.
5. Top with the remaining non-condiment-topped slices of toast.
6. Cut each sandwich in half, or in quarters if desired.

Nutrition Information:
Calories: 303, Total Fat: 17.8g, Saturated Fat: 3.9g, Cholesterol: 34.5mg,
Sodium: 437.4mg, Carbohydrates: 23.4g, Fiber: 5.4g, Protein: 14.8g

47. Spinach and Feta Quiche

Spinach and Feta Quiche is a hearty and delicious quiche perfect for any
occasion. The two main ingredients, spinach and feta, are both naturally
packed with flavour, making it a delicious and nutritious option. This
quiche recipe serves 8 people and takes approximately 20 minutes to
prepare, with a ready time of 45 minutes.
Serving: 8
| Preparation Time: 20 minutes
| Ready Time: 45 minutes

Ingredients:
1. 3 large eggs
2. 1 cup of heavy cream
3. 1/4 teaspoon of ground nutmeg
4. 1 teaspoon of garlic powder
5. 1/2 teaspoon of salt
6. 1/2 teaspoon of ground black pepper
7. 1/2 cup of chopped onions
8. 1 1/2 cups of chopped cooked spinach
9. 3/4 cup of crumbled feta cheese
10. 1 9-inch unbaked deep-dish pie crust

Instructions:
1. Preheat the oven to 375F.
2. In a large bowl, whisk together the eggs, cream, nutmeg, garlic
powder, salt and pepper.
3. Stir in the onions, spinach and feta cheese until well combined.
4. Pour the mixture into the unbaked pie crust.
5. Bake for 40 to 45 minutes, or until the center is set and the top is
golden brown.
6. Let cool for 10 minutes before serving.

Nutrition Information:
Per serving: 280 calories, 20g fat, 10g carbohydrates, 14g protein

48. Sweet Potato and Lentil Stew

Sweet Potato and Lentil Stew is a hearty and healthy vegan stew with an array of spices and flavors. It is an easy to make and budget friendly meal that can be ready in just an hour and perfect for a hearty dinner.
Serving: Serves 4
| Preparation Time: 10 minutes
| Ready Time: 1 hour

Ingredients:
· 2 tablespoons olive oil
· 1 onion, chopped
· 1 garlic clove, minced
· 1 teaspoon ground cumin
· 1 teaspoon smoked paprika
· 1 teaspoon ground coriander
· A pinch of ground red pepper
· 1 (14-ounce) can diced tomatoes
· 1/2 teaspoon sea salt
· 4 cups vegetable broth
· 1 cup dried green lentils
· 1 large sweet potato, peeled and cubed
· 2 cups chopped spinach

Instructions:
1. Heat oil in a large pot on medium heat.
2. Add onion and garlic, stir and cook until soft.
3. Add cumin, smoked paprika, ground coriander, and red pepper. Stir and cook for 1 minute.
4. Add diced tomatoes, sea salt, and vegetable broth. Stir and bring to a simmer.
5. Add lentils and sweet potatoes. Cook for 25 minutes or until lentils are tender.
6. Add spinach and cook for another 5 minutes.
7. Serve warm.

Nutrition Information:
Approximately 161 calories per serving, 5.7 grams of fat, 25grams of carbohydrates, and 6.1 grams of protein per serving.

49. Tuna and White Bean Salad

This simple and nutritious Tuna and White Bean Salad only requires a few ingredients and is a quick, easy meal to make. It is high in protein and low in carbohydrates, making it a great choice for lunch or dinner.
Serving: 4
| Preparation Time: 10 minutes
| Ready Time: 10 minutes

Ingredients:
- 2 cans (5 oz) of low-sodium canned tuna, drained
- 2 cans (15.5 oz) of cannellini beans, drained and rinsed
- 2 carrots, grated
- 2 stalks of celery, diced
- 2 tablespoons extra-virgin olive oil
- Juice of 1 lemon
- 2 teaspoons of fresh parsley, minced
- Salt and pepper to taste

Instructions:
1. In a large bowl, combine the drained tuna and beans.
2. Add the grated carrots, diced celery, olive oil, lemon juice, and parsley to the bowl.
3. Mix the salad together before season with salt and pepper to taste.
4. Divide the salad among four plates and serve.

Nutrition Information:
Serving Size: 1
Calories: 145
Total Fat: 6g
Saturated Fat: 1g
Cholesterol: 38mg
Sodium: 164mg

Total Carbohydrates: 11g
Dietary Fiber: 4g
Protein: 12g

50. Grilled Chicken and Vegetable Skewers

Grilled Chicken and Vegetable Skewers are a delicious and healthy meal filled with juicy grilled chicken and fresh vegetables on a skewer--perfect for a summer day! This dish is quick and easy to make and is sure to please a crowd.

Serving: 4
| Preparation Time: 15 minutes
| Ready Time: 20 minutes

Ingredients:
• 1 lb. Chicken Tenderloins, cut into 1-inch cubes
• 2 cups Assorted Vegetables (zucchini, mushrooms, red pepper, red onion), cut into 1-inch cubes
• 1/4 cup Olive Oil
• 1 teaspoon Salt
• 2 teaspoons Black Pepper
• 1 teaspoon Garlic Powder
• Wooden Skewers

Instructions:
1. Preheat the grill or grill pan to medium high heat.
2. Place chicken and vegetables in a large bowl and add olive oil, salt, pepper, garlic powder. Toss until everything is evenly coated.
3. Thread the chicken and vegetables onto skewers covering each skewer equally.
4. Grill for about 10 minutes, turning occasionally, until chicken is cooked through and vegetables are tender.

Nutrition Information (per serving):
Calories: 241
Protein: 23g
Carbohydrates: 6g
Fat: 12g

51. Chicken and Black Bean Burrito Bowl

This Chicken and Black Bean Burrito Bowl is absolutely delicious! Bursting with flavor, this Mexican-inspired entrée is sure to please the whole family. Everyone will love it!
Serving: 4-6
| Preparation Time: 15 minutes
| Ready Time: 30 minutes

Ingredients:
- 2 tsp olive oil
- 1 onion, diced
- 2 cloves garlic, minced
- 1 jalapeno pepper, seeded and minced
- 1 lb boneless skinless chicken breasts, diced
- 1 tsp chili powder
- 1 tsp ground cumin
- 1/2 cup chicken broth
- 1 can black beans, rinsed and drained
- 1/2 cup frozen corn
- 1/2 cup salsa
- 1/2 cup sour cream
- 4-6 large burrito-size whole wheat flour tortillas
- Shredded cheddar cheese
- Chopped fresh cilantro

Instructions:
1. Heat olive oil in a large skillet over medium heat. Add the onion and garlic and sauté for 3 minutes.
2. Add jalapeno pepper and chicken breast and cook for about 6 minutes, stirring occasionally.
3. Add chili powder and cumin, stirring for about 1 minute.
4. Add chicken broth, black beans, and corn, stirring and cooking for about 8 minutes or until chicken is cooked through.
5. Add salsa, sour cream, and heat through.
6. Remove from heat and serve over 4 to 6 warmed tortillas.
7. Top with shredded cheese and cilantro.

Nutrition Information:
Per Serving (without toppings):
Calories: 310, Total fat: 5.6g, Saturated fat: 1.8g, Cholesterol: 57mg,
Sodium: 615mg, Carbohydrates: 35.6g, Fiber: 7.7g, Protein: 24.7g

52. Quinoa and Vegetable Stuffed Peppers

This delicious, nutritious dish of Quinoa and Vegetable Stuffed Peppers
is easy to make and full of flavor. Enjoy it for a quick and filling lunch or
dinner.
Serving: 4-6
| Preparation Time: 10 minutes
| Ready Time: 45 minutes

Ingredients:
- 4 large bell peppers
- 1 cup quinoa
- 2 tablespoons olive oil
- 1 onion, diced
- 2 cloves garlic, minced
- 1 zucchini, diced
- 1 tomato, diced
- 2 cups vegetable broth
- 1 teaspoon oregano
- Salt and pepper, to taste
- 1/2 cup feta cheese

Instructions:
1. Preheat oven to 375F.
2. Cut tops off of peppers, remove seeds and vein, and then set aside.
3. Bring quinoa and vegetable broth to a boil in a saucepan and then
reduce heat to low. Simmer, covered, for 15 minutes, or until quinoa is
cooked through.
4. Meanwhile, heat olive oil in a large skillet over medium heat. Add
onion, garlic, and zucchini, and cook for 5 minutes, stirring occasionally.
Add tomato, oregano, salt, and pepper, and cook for another 5 minutes.
5. Add cooked quinoa and feta to the pan and stir to combine.

6. Stuff peppers with quinoa mixture and place in a baking dish. Pour any remaining quinoa mixture around peppers.

7. Bake for 30 minutes, or until peppers are tender.

Nutrition Information:
Serving size: 1 stuffed pepper
Calories: 245
Protein: 10g
Carbohydrates: 34g
Fat: 10g
Cholesterol: 4mg
Sodium: 333mg
Fiber: 7g
Sugar: 5g

53. Zucchini Noodle Bowl with Chicken

This Zucchini Noodle Bowl with Chicken is a simple yet flavorful one-dish meal. Loaded with vegetables, protein, and herbs, this is an easy and healthy family favorite.

Serving: 4
| Preparation Time: 10 minutes
| Ready Time: 15 minutes

Ingredients:
• 2 tablespoons olive oil
• 1 garlic clove, minced
• 1/2 cup chopped onions
• 2 tablespoons lemon juice
• 1 pound boneless skinless chicken breast, cut into 1 inch pieces
• 1 teaspoon oregano
• Salt and pepper to taste
• 3 zucchinis, spiralized
• 1 tomato, chopped
• 1/4 cup fresh basil, sliced

Instructions:
1. Heat oil in a large skillet over medium heat.

2. Add garlic and onion and sauté for 1 minute.

3. Add chicken, lemon juice, oregano, salt and pepper and cook until chicken is browned and cooked through.

4. Add zucchini noodles and tomato to the skillet and cook for 2-3 minutes or until zucchini is tender.

5. Taste and adjust seasoning if desired.

6. Serve in shallow bowls and top with fresh basil.

Nutrition Information:
• Calories: 181
• Carbohydrates: 8.2 g
• Protein: 20.6 g
• Fat: 7.8 g
• Sodium: 108.2 mg

54. Veggiealoaded Shepherd's Pie

Veggiealoaded Shepherd's Pie is a healthy, delicious and easy-to-make meal, filled with nutrient-rich veggies and a flavorful mash potato topping - perfect for a cozy evening at home.

Serving: 6-8

Prep Time: 20 mins

| Ready Time: 1 hour

Ingredients:
- 2 tablespoons olive oil
- 1 onion, chopped
- 2 cloves garlic, minced
- 2 stalks of celery, chopped
- 2 carrots, chopped
- 1 teaspoon cumin
- 1 teaspoon paprika
- 1/4 teaspoon dried thyme
- 2 cups vegetable broth
- 1 (14.5 ounce) can diced tomatoes, undrained
- 2 tablespoons tomato paste
- 4 cups mixed frozen vegetables, thawed
- 2 tablespoons dairy-free margarine

- 2 tablespoons all-purpose flour
- 2 tablespoons dairy-free milk
- 2 cups mashed potatoes
- 1/4 cup vegan cheese shreds
- 2 tablespoons diced fresh parsley
- Salt and freshly ground pepper, to taste

Instructions:
1. Preheat oven to 375° F.
2. In a large skillet, heat oil over medium heat. Add onion and garlic and cook until fragrant, 3 minutes.
3. Add celery and carrots and cook, stirring occasionally, until softened, 5 minutes.
4. Add cumin, paprika, thyme and vegetable broth and stir to combine. Simmer, stirring occasionally, until vegetables are tender, 8 minutes.
5. Add tomatoes and tomato paste and stir to combine. Simmer, stirring occasionally, until thickened, 5 minutes.
6. Add mixed vegetables and stir to combine. Cook until heated through, 3 minutes.
7. Transfer vegetable mixture to baking dish.
8. In a small saucepan, melt margarine over medium heat. Add flour and stir to combine. Cook flour mixture, stirring constantly, until golden and fragrant, 3 minutes.
9. Remove from heat and slowly stir in dairy-free milk until fully combined.
10. Return saucepan to heat and cook, stirring constantly, until thickened, 2 minutes.
11. Remove from heat and stir in mashed potatoes until fully combined.
12. Spread mashed potato mixture over vegetable mixture in baking dish.
13. Sprinkle vegan cheese shreds over mashed potatoes and bake, uncovered, until golden and bubbling, 30 minutes. Sprinkle with parsley and season with salt and pepper.

Nutrition Information:
Calories: 211kcal, Carbohydrates: 30g, Protein: 7.6g, Fat: 7.7g, Saturated Fat: 2.6g, Polyunsaturated Fat: 4.1g, Monounsaturated Fat: 0.9g, Sodium: 486mg, Potassium: 464mg, Fiber: 6.2g, Sugar: 7.6g, Vitamin A: 7115IU, Vitamin C: 59.8mg, Calcium: 46mg, Iron: 2.3mg

55. Thai Peanut Chicken Wraps

These tasty Thai Peanut Chicken Wraps feature a spiced peanut sauce, crunchy red bell peppers, and juicy grilled chicken. They are perfect for a summer dinner or as a party appetizer!
Serving: Makes 8 wraps
| Preparation Time: 15 Minutes
| Ready Time: 25 minutes

Ingredients:
- 8 small/medium tortillas
- 2 tablespoons olive oil
- 2 teaspoons garlic, minced
- 2 boneless, skinless chicken breasts, cut in thin strips
- 1 red bell pepper, julienned
- 2 tablespoons low-sodium soy sauce
- 1 teaspoon crushed red pepper
- 1/2 cup creamy peanut butter
- juice from 1 lime
- 1 teaspoon agave nectar
- 1/4 cup fresh basil, chopped

Instructions:
1. Heat olive oil in large skillet over medium heat.
2. Add garlic and chicken strips and cook, stirring occasionally, until chicken is cooked through, about 8 minutes.
3. Add bell pepper, soy sauce, and crushed red pepper; continue cooking until bell pepper is softened, about 5 minutes
4. In a small bowl, whisk together peanut butter, lime juice, agave nectar, and basil.
5. Add sauce to skillet and stir to combine.
6. Place about 1/4 cup of chicken mixture in the center of each tortilla and roll it up.
7. Serve immediately.

Nutrition Information:
(per wrap) 190 Calories, 9g Fat, 13g Protein, 15g Carbohydrates, 3g Fiber, 4g Sugar

56. Greek Chickpea Salad

This vibrant, healthy Greek Chickpea Salad is a flavor-packed side dish that's ready in just 20 minutes. Perfect for barbecues, summer picnics, and potlucks!
Serving: 4 people
| Preparation Time: 10 minutes
| Ready Time: 20 minutes

Ingredients:
- 2 cans Chickpeas (15.5 oz each), drained and rinsed
- 1/2 small Red Onion, diced
- 1/2 large Cucumber, diced
- 1/3 cup Kalamata Olives, pitted and diced
- 2 Roma Tomatoes, diced
- 2 tablespoons Parsley, chopped
- 2 tablespoons Olive Oil
- 2 tablespoons Lemon Juice
- 2 cloves Garlic, minced
- 1/4 teaspoon Salt
- 1/4 teaspoon Black Pepper

Instructions:
1. In a bowl, combine chickpeas, red onion, cucumber, olives, tomatoes and parsley.
2. In a separate bowl, whisk together olive oil, lemon juice, garlic, salt and pepper.
3. Pour dressing over chickpea mixture and stir to combine.
4. Serve immediately or refrigerate for later.

Nutrition Information:
Serving Size: 1 cup
Calories: 200 kcal, Carbohydrates: 17 g, Protein: 5 g, Fat: 13 g, Saturated Fat: 2 g, Sodium: 408 mg, Potassium: 305 mg, Fiber: 6 g, Sugar: 2 g, Vitamin A: 712 IU, Vitamin C: 14 mg, Calcium: 44 mg, Iron: 2 mg

57. Egg and Avocado Toast

Egg and Avocado Toast is a savory dish that combines creamy avocado and protein-packed eggs into a hearty and delicious open-faced sandwich. It's perfect for a quick meal any time of the day!
Serving: 2
| Preparation Time: 10 minutes
| Ready Time: 10 minutes

Ingredients:
- 4 slices of your favorite toast
- 2 eggs
- 1 medium avocado
- 2 tablespoons of plain Greek yogurt
- 2 tablespoons of olive oil
- 1/4 teaspoon of paprika
- Salt and black pepper to taste

Instructions:
1. Preheat a nonstick skillet over medium heat and add the olive oil.
2. Toast your bread to your desired level of crispiness.
3. Crack the two eggs into the skillet and season them with paprika, salt, and pepper. Cook until the whites are firm and the yolks begin to thicken.
4. Mash the avocado with the Greek yogurt in a bowl.
5. Spread the avocado mixture onto the toast.
6. Place the eggs over the avocado and season again with additional salt and pepper.

Nutrition Information:
Serving: 2, Calories: 310, Total Fat: 19g, Saturated Fat: 3g, Trans Fat: 0g, Unsaturated Fat: 15g, Cholesterol: 169mg, Sodium: 413mg, Carbohydrates: $25g$, Fiber: 8g, Sugar: 4g, Protein: 12g

58. Tempeh and Vegetable Kebabs

Tempeh and Vegetable Kebabs are a delicious and healthy vegan meal. With a variety of plant-based ingredients like tempeh, mushrooms, bell peppers and more, these kebabs are full of flavor and nutrition.
Serving: 5-6

| Preparation Time: 10 minutes
| Ready Time: 25 minutes

Ingredients:
-1 8-ounce package of tempeh, cut into small cubes
-1 onion, diced
-1 red bell pepper, diced
-1 yellow bell pepper, diced
-2 cloves garlic, minced
-1 tablespoon olive oil
-2 tablespoons soy sauce
-4-5 white mushrooms, finely chopped
-1 teaspoon dried oregano
-Salt and pepper, to taste
-Wooden skewers

Instructions:
1. Preheat oven to 400 degrees Fahrenheit.
2. In a bowl, combine cubed tempeh, diced onion, diced bell peppers, minced garlic, olive oil, soy sauce, finely chopped mushrooms and oregano.
3. Mix to combine, then season with salt and pepper.
4. Thread cubes of tempeh and vegetables onto wooden skewers.
5. Place kebabs on a greased baking sheet and bake in preheated oven for 15-20 minutes, flipping once halfway through.
6. Once cooked, serve with a side of your choice and enjoy!

Nutrition Information (per serving):
Calories: 267
Fat: 14.7 g
Carbohydrates: 14.2 g
Protein: 21.9 g
Fiber: 3.3 g

59. Baked Eggplant Parmesan

Baked Eggplant Parmesan is a delicious Italian-inspired dish with layers of eggplant, cheese, and marinara sauce all cooked together to perfection. Serves 8. | Preparation Time 10 minutes. Ready time 40 minutes.

Ingredients:
- 2 large eggplants, sliced into 1/2 inch thick slices
- 2 cups mozzarella cheese, shredded
- 1 cup Parmesan cheese, grated
- 2 cups marinara sauce
- 2 tablespoons olive oil
- 2 tablespoons Italian seasoning
- 1 teaspoon garlic powder
- Salt and pepper, to taste

Instructions:
1. Preheat oven to 375 degrees F and prepare a 9x13 inch baking dish.
2. Place the eggplant slices in a single layer in the baking dish.
3. Drizzle olive oil over the eggplant slices and season with salt and pepper.
4. In a separate bowl, combine the Italian seasoning, garlic powder, and Parmesan cheese.
5. Sprinkle the cheese mixture over the eggplant slices evenly.
6. Top with marinara sauce and mozzarella cheese.
7. Bake at 375 degrees F for 30 minutes, or until the cheese is melted and the eggplant is cooked through.
8. Serve warm.

Nutrition Information:
Calories: 280, Total Fat: 17.2g, Saturated Fat: 6.6g, Cholesterol: 22mg, Sodium: 477mg, Total Carbohydrates: 17.5g, Dietary Fiber: 4.4g, Protein: 14.4g

60. Shrimp and Broccoli Stir-fry

Shrimp and Broccoli Stir-fry is a healthy and flavorful Chinese-inspired dish. It features marinated shrimp and plenty of vegetables that are stir-fried in a savory soy sauce. Serve it over cooked brown rice or noodles for a filling and tasty meal.

Serving: 4
| Preparation Time: 10 minutes
| Ready Time: 20 minutes

Ingredients:
- 1/2 lb large shrimp, peeled and deveined
- 2 cloves garlic, minced
- 2 tablespoons soy sauce, divided
- 1 teaspoon sesame oil
- 1 head broccoli, cut into florets
- 2 tablespoons vegetable oil
- Salt and pepper, to taste

Instructions:
1. In a medium bowl, combine shrimp, garlic, 1 tablespoon soy sauce, and sesame oil. Cover and marinate in the refrigerator for 10 minutes.
2. Heat vegetable oil in a large skillet over medium-high heat. Add shrimp, and season with salt and pepper. Cook until shrimp is cooked through, about 3 minutes.
3. Add the broccoli florets, and the remaining tablespoon of soy sauce. Stir-fry until the broccoli is crisp-tender and the shrimp is cooked through, about 5 minutes.

Nutrition Information (per serving):
Calories: 159 calories; Protein: 18.4g; Total Fat: 8.4g; Sodium: 751mg; Total Carbohydrate: 4.4g; Fiber: 1.5g

61. Chickpea and Spinach Soup

This delicious and filling vegan Chickpea and Spinach Soup is a great way to get in some important health-boosting nutrients. A combination of warm flavors, a rich texture and comforting warmth make this soup a great choice for lunch or dinner.
Serving: 6
| Preparation Time: 10 minutes
| Ready Time: 30 minutes

Ingredients:

- 1 tablespoon olive oil
- 1 onion, diced
- 2 cloves garlic, minced
- 2 carrots, diced
- 2 stalks celery, diced
- 2 (15-ounce) cans chickpeas, drained and rinsed
- 6 cups vegetable broth
- 1 teaspoon dried oregano
- 1/2 teaspoon ground cumin
- 1/2 teaspoon smoked paprika
- 2 cups baby spinach

Instructions:
1. Heat the oil in a large pot over medium-high heat. Add the onion, garlic, carrots, and celery and cook, stirring frequently, for about 5 minutes, or until the onion is translucent.
2. Add the chickpeas, vegetable broth, oregano, cumin, and smoked paprika and bring the mixture to a boil.
3. Reduce the heat to low and simmer the soup for 15 minutes.
4. Add in the spinach and simmer for an additional 5 minutes.
5. Serve hot.

Nutrition Information:
Calories: 248
Total Fat: 4.3g
Saturated Fat: 0.6g
Carbohydrates: 37.3g
Protein: 11.3g
Fiber: 11g

62. Quinoa and Avocado Salad

This refreshing and energizing Quinoa and Avocado Salad is a delicious and healthy meal that is excellent for lunch or dinner. Packed with nutritious ingredients, it is a great way to get your daily dose of protein and vegetables.
Serving: 4

| Preparation Time: 15 minutes
| Ready Time: 25 minutes

Ingredients:
- 1 cup uncooked quinoa
- 2 cups vegetable broth
- 2 ripe avocados, chopped
- 1 small red onion, diced
- 2 cloves garlic, minced
- 2 tablespoons olive oil
- 2 tablespoons apple cider vinegar
- Salt and pepper, to taste
- 2 tablespoons freshly squeezed lime juice
- 1/2 cup cherry tomatoes, halved
- 2 tablespoons fresh cilantro, finely chopped

Instructions:
1. Begin by cooking the quinoa. In a medium saucepan, bring the vegetable broth to a boil. Stir in quinoa, reduce heat to low, cover, and simmer for 15 minutes or until all liquid is absorbed.
2. In a separate medium bowl, combine the avocado, onion, garlic, olive oil, vinegar, salt, pepper, and lime juice. Gently stir to combine.
3. Once the quinoa is ready, fluff with a fork, then transfer to the bowl with the avocado mixture. Gently stir to combine.
4. Add the halved cherry tomatoes and chopped cilantro. Stir to combine.

Nutrition Information:
Serving size: 1/4 of recipe
Calories: 190, Fat: 11.2 g, Sat. Fat: 1.5 g, Cholesterol: 0 mg, Sodium: 118 mg, Carbs: 19.4 g, Fiber: 4.7 g, Sugar: 1.8 g, Protein: 4.5 g

63. Baked Falafel with Tahini Sauce

Everyone loves falafels, and this delicious baked version with a tahini sauce is a vegetarian favorite. A winning combination of fiber-rich garbanzo beans and flavorful spices, this falafel makes for a satisfying entrée or side, ready in about an hour.

Serving: Serves 8
| Preparation Time: 15 minutes
| Ready Time: 45 minutes

Ingredients:
- 2 (15.5-ounce) cans garbanzo beans, rinsed and drained
- 1/2 cup grated onion
- 1/2 cup chopped fresh parsley or cilantro
- 1/2 teaspoon ground cumin
- 1/2 teaspoon garlic powder
- 1/4 teaspoon ground black pepper
- 1/4 teaspoon baking soda
- Salt to taste
- 2 tablespoons cold-pressed olive oil
- For the tahini sauce:
- 1/2 cup tahini
- Juice of 1 lemon
- 1 medium-sized clove garlic, minced
- Salt and ground black pepper, to taste
- Water as needed (for desired consistency)

Instructions:
1. Preheat oven to 375F (190°C).
2. Place garbanzo beans, grated onion, parsley or cilantro, cumin, garlic powder, black pepper, baking soda, and salt in bowl of a food processor. Pulse several times until ingredients are blended but still retain some texture (not a paste).
3. Scoop out spoonfuls of the mixture and shape into patties. Place on baking sheet lined with parchment paper and brush tops with olive oil.
4. Bake for 25 minutes, flipping halfway through.
5. Meanwhile, in a medium-sized bowl, mix together tahini, lemon juice, garlic, salt, pepper, and water until creamy and lightly drizzled, adding more water as needed to reach desired consistency.
6. Top baked falafels with tahini sauce and serve hot.

Nutrition Information:
Per serving: 160 calories, 8g fat, 17g carbs, 4g protein, 4g fiber, 260mg sodium.

64. Spinach and Cheddar Quinoa Cakes

Spinach and Cheddar Quinoa cakes are a savoury, flavorful dish that is sure to be a hit with family and friends. Filled with wholesome quinoa, fresh spinach and cheddar cheese, these cakes are both delicious and nutritious.

Serving: 8-10 cakes
| Preparation Time: 10 minutes
| Ready Time: 25 minutes

Ingredients:
- 2 cups cooked quinoa
- 1/4 cup grated cheddar cheese
- 1/4 cup grated parmesan cheese
- 2 eggs, lightly beaten
- 2 garlic cloves, minced
- 2 tablespoons all-purpose flour
- 2 tablespoons olive oil
- 2 cups fresh baby spinach leaves
- Salt and pepper to taste

Instruction:
1. Preheat the oven to 375F/190°C. Grease a baking sheet with non-stick spray.
2. In a large bowl, combine the cooked quinoa, cheddar cheese, parmesan cheese, eggs, garlic, flour, olive oil, and spinach. Season with salt and pepper as desired.
3. Form the quinoa mixture into 8-10 small patties, about 2" across, and place on the greased baking sheet.
4. Bake in the oven for 20-25 minutes, or until golden brown. Serve hot.

Nutrition Information (per serving):
Calories: 230 kcal
Total Fat: 13g
Saturated Fat: 3.7g
Cholesterol: 77mg
Sodium: 530mg
Carbohydrates: 17.3g
Fiber: 2.5g
Sugar: 0.6g

Protein: 11g

65. Turkey and Sweet Potato Patties

Turkey and Sweet Potato Patties are a delicious and healthy meal packed with flavor and protein. This savory dish is infused with parsley, garlic, and onion and is sure to be a hit with the whole family. Serve alongside a fresh salad for a complete meal.

Serving: 4
| Preparation Time: 15 minutes
| Ready Time: 40 minutes

Ingredients:
- 2 pounds ground turkey
- 1 large sweet potato, peeled and grated
- 1 large yellow onion, grated
- 2 cloves garlic, diced
- 1 egg
- 3 tablespoons fresh parsley, chopped
- 2 teaspoons chili powder
- 2 teaspoons ground cumin
- 1/2 teaspoon ground black pepper
- 1/4 teaspoon sea salt
- 1 tablespoon olive oil

Instructions:
1. Preheat oven to 375F.
2. In a medium mixing bowl, add the ground turkey, sweet potato, onion, garlic, egg, parsley, chili powder, cumin, black pepper, and salt.
3. Stir well until all ingredients are combined.
4. Using your hands, shape the mixture into eight patties and place on a parchment-lined baking sheet.
5. Drizzle olive oil over the patties.
6. Bake for 25 minutes, or until the internal temperature reaches 165F.

Nutrition Information (per serving):
326 calories, 15g fat, 12g carbohydrates, 37g protein.

66. Salmon and Potato Salmon Poke Bowl

Salmon and Potato Salmon Poke Bowl is a nutritious and delicious meal that is perfect for any lunch or dinner. This bowl is easy to make and only requires a few simple ingredients.
Serves: 4, | Preparation Time: 10 minutes, | Ready Time: 25 minutes.

Ingredients:
-1 pound diced salmon
-1/2 cup diced onions
-1/2 cup diced avocado
-1 cup cooked and diced potatoes
-1/4 cup soy sauce
-1 tablespoon honey
-1 teaspoon sesame oil
-2 tablespoons toasted white sesame seeds
-1/2 cup cooked sushi rice
-1/4 cup pickled ginger
-1/4 cup edamame

Instructions:
1. Preheat the oven to 375 degrees F.
2. In a large bowl, combine the diced salmon, diced onions, diced avocado, cooked and diced potatoes, soy sauce, honey, and sesame oil.
3. Spread the mixture onto a baking sheet and bake for 15 minutes.
4. While the salmon and potatoes are baking, combine the cooked sushi rice, pickled ginger, and edamame in a separate bowl.
5. Once the salmon and potatoes are done baking, combine them with the rice, ginger, and edamame.
6. Serve the Salmon Poke Bowl with toasted white sesame seeds and some extra soy sauce, if desired.

Nutrition Information:
Calories: 310, Fat: 10g, Carbohydrates: 26g, Protein: 24g, Dietary Fiber: 3g, Sodium: 566mg

67. Tuna Nicoise Salad

Tuna Nicoise Salad is a classic French dish, perfect for a light lunch or dinner. An ideal combination of refreshing greens and canned tuna, this salad is a delicious and nutritious meal.

Serving: 4 | | Preparation Time: 10 minutes | | Ready Time: 10 minutes.

Ingredients:
- 2 x 185 Grams canned tuna
- 2 cups chopped green beans
- 2 cups cooked potatoes, cubed
- 2 cooked eggs, cut in half
- 1 cup cherry tomatoes, halved
- 1/4 cup black olives, sliced
- 2 tablespoons white balsamic vinegar
- 80 ml olive oil
- Salt and pepper, to taste

Instructions:
1. In a large bowl, combine the tuna, green beans, potatoes, eggs, tomatoes, and olives.
2. In a small bowl, whisk together the white balsamic vinegar and olive oil.
3. Dress the salad with the dressing and season with salt and pepper, to taste.
4. Serve chilled or at room temperature.

Nutrition Information:
Calories: 400.2 kcal, Total Fat: 23 g, Sodium: 300 mg, Total Carbohydrates: 18.5 g, Protein: 25.9 g.

68. Mediterranean Veggie Wrap

For a light and healthy lunch, try this Mediterranean Veggie Wrap! Packed with delicious, fresh ingredients, this wrap is sure to be a hit.

Serving: 4
| Preparation Time: 10 minutes

| Ready Time: 10 minutes

Ingredients:
- 4 wraps of your choice
- 2 cups romaine lettuce, chopped
- 1/2 cup cherry tomatoes, halved
- 1/4 red onion, thinly sliced
- 2 avocados, sliced
- 2 tbsp olive oil
- 2 tbsp red wine vinegar
- 1/4 cup kalamata olives, halved
- Salt & pepper to taste

Instructions:
1. In a large bowl, combine the lettuce, tomatoes, onion, avocado and olives.
2. In a smaller bowl, whisk together the olive oil, red wine vinegar, salt and pepper.
3. Drizzle the dressing over the veggies and gently toss to combine.
4. Divide the veggie mixture into 4 parts and spread the mixture onto each wrap.
5. Fold the wrap and cut in half.

Nutrition Information: (per wrap)
240 calories, 10g fat, 9g protein, 36g carbohydrates

69. Baked Salmon Burger

Baked Salmon Burger is a delicious and healthy alternative to traditional beef burgers. With a simple | Preparation Time of 20 minutes and ready time of 20 minutes, this dish makes a perfect and easy weeknight meal. Serving: Serves 2
| Preparation Time: 20 minutes
| Ready Time: 20 minutes

Ingredients:
- 2x 4oz salmon fillets
- 2 cups crushed crackers

- Garlic powder to taste
- Salt and pepper to taste
- 2 tsp olive oil

Instructions:
1. Preheat oven to 375F.
2. Mix crushed crackers, garlic powder, salt, and pepper in a bowl.
3. Dip salmon fillets into bowl and coat completely with the cracker mixture.
4. Place salmon burgers onto a baking sheet and lightly brush tops of each fillet with olive oil.
5. Bake for 15 minutes and then broil for 5 minutes, until the tops of the burgers are golden brown in color.
6. Serve and enjoy on a bun or as is.

Nutrition Information:
-Calories: 305
-Total Fat: 13 g
-Saturated Fat: 3 g
-Protein: 23 g
-Carbohydrates: 20 g
-Fiber: 2 g

70. Curried Veggie Buddha Bowl

This Curried Veggie Buddha Bowl is a quick and easy meal option full of flavorful veggies. It's a great vegan-friendly choice that can be served either hot or cold.
Serving: 2
| Preparation Time: 15 minutes
| Ready Time: 20 minutes

Ingredients:
- 2 tablespoons extra-virgin olive oil
- 1/2 large red onion, chopped
- 1 red bell pepper, chopped
- 1 cup cauliflower florets
- 1 teaspoon curry powder

- Salt and black pepper
- 1 cup cooked brown rice
- 4 ounces firm tofu, cubed
- 1/2 cup canned chickpeas
- 1/2 cup plain Greek yogurt
- 1 tablespoon freshly chopped cilantro leaves
- 1 tablespoon freshly chopped mint leaves

Instructions:
1. Heat the oil in a large skillet over medium-high heat.
2. Add the onion, bell pepper and cauliflower to the skillet and sauté for 3 to 4 minutes, until the vegetables are tender and lightly browned.
3. Stir in the curry powder, salt and black pepper.
4. Add the cooked rice, tofu and chickpeas and cook and stir for an additional 2 minutes.
5. Divide the mixture in half and serve each portion in a bowl topped with the Greek yogurt, cilantro and mint leaves.

Nutrition Information:
Calories - 315
Fat - 8.9g
Carbohydrates - 39.5g
Protein - 17.4g

71. Tofu and Vegetable Stir-Fry

Tofu and Vegetable Stir-Fry is a flavorful and nourishing dish that combines healthy vegetables with seasoned tofu. This delicious vegan dish is easy to prepare and can be served as a side dish or entree.
Serving: 4
| Preparation Time: 10 minutes
| Ready Time: 20 minutes

Ingredients:
• 14 ounces extra-firm tofu, cubed
• 2 tablespoons soy sauce
• 1 tablespoon sesame oil
• 2 cloves of garlic, minced

- 2 tablespoons fresh ginger, grated
- 1 red bell pepper, sliced into strips
- 1 zucchini, cut into half-moons
- 1 cup broccoli florets
- 2 tablespoons vegetable oil

Instructions:
1. In a large bowl, combine soy sauce, sesame oil, garlic, and ginger.
2. Add the tofu cubes to the mixture and toss to coat. Set aside.
3. Heat the vegetable oil in a large skillet over medium-high heat.
4. Add the bell pepper, zucchini, and broccoli and cook until tender, about 5 minutes.
5. Add the tofu mixture and cook until heated through, about 5 minutes more.

Nutrition Information:
per serving (1/4 of the dish): Calories: 230, Fat: 12g, Saturated Fat: 1.5g, Cholesterol: 0mg, Sodium: 630mg, Carbohydrates: 15g, Fiber: 4g, Sugar: 4g, Protein: 17g.

72. Turkey and Zucchini Fritters

Turkey and Zucchini Fritters are a delicious, crunchy and healthy snack that packs plenty of flavor. Made with ground turkey and shredded zucchini, the combination of these two ingredients makes for a high protein, low carb and nutrient-packed meal. Serve these fritters as an appetizer or as a main course.
Serving: 8
| Preparation Time: 15 minutes
| Ready Time: 40 minutes

Ingredients:
- 2 lbs ground turkey
- 2 zucchinis, shredded
- 2 cloves garlic, minced
- 1/2 cup onion, chopped
- 1 teaspoon salt
- 1 teaspoon black pepper

- 1/2 teaspoon paprika
- 1/4 cup parsley, finely chopped
- 2 large eggs
- 1/2 cup all-purpose flour
- 2 tablespoons olive oil

Instructions

1. In a large bowl, mix together the ground turkey, zucchini, garlic, onion, salt, pepper and paprika.
2. Next, add the eggs and flour and knead with your hands until everything is well combined.
3. Heat a large skillet over medium heat and add the olive oil.
4. Using a spoon, form 2-3 inch patties with the turkey mixture and place them in the hot skillet.
5. Fry each side of the patties for 5-7 minutes or until golden brown.
6. Serve the Turkey and Zucchini Fritters with your favorite dipping sauce.

Nutrition Information (per serving):
Calories: 232
Total Fat: 12 g
Saturated Fat: 2 g
Cholesterol: 104 mg
Sodium: 282 mg
Carbohydrates: 8 g
Fiber: 1 g
Protein: 21 g

73. Soba Noodle Bowl with Chicken

Soba Noodle Bowl with Chicken is a hearty and delicious way to fill up on a busy weeknight. The savory flavors of the teriyaki-marinated chicken, accompanied by soft soba noodles and crunchy vegetables, make this meal truly satisfying. Serve this bowl as a complete one-dish meal.
Serving: 4
| Preparation Time: 15 minutes
| Ready Time: 45 minutes

Ingredients:
- 1 lb boneless, skinless chicken thighs
- 1/3 cup low-sodium teriyaki sauce
- 6 cups chicken broth
- 8 oz dried soba noodles
- 2 cups broccoli florets
- 1 red bell pepper, diced
- 2 cloves garlic, minced
- 3 green onions, thinly sliced
- 2 tablespoons sesame oil
- Salt and pepper, to taste

Instructions:
1. Preheat oven to 375F and line a baking sheet with aluminum foil.
2. Put chicken thighs in a bowl and pour teriyaki sauce over, tossing to coat. Transfer chicken thighs to prepared baking sheet.
3. Bake for 25 minutes, or until cooked through.
4. While chicken is baking, bring the chicken broth to a boil in a large pot. Add soba noodles, broccoli, and red bell pepper and reduce heat to low. Simmer for 10 minutes, or until soba noodles are cooked through.
5. Remove chicken from the oven and cut into thin slices.
6. Add garlic, green onions, and sesame oil to the pot and stir to combine.
7. Add cooked chicken and season with salt and pepper, to taste.
8. Serve and enjoy!

Nutrition Information:
Per Serving: 485 calories, 21g fat, 29g carbohydrates, 36g protein.

74. Roasted Veggie and Lentil Salad

Roasted Veggie and Lentil Salad is the perfect combination of smoky and savory flavors! This delicious and healthy dish is packed with roasted vegetables, lentils, and herbs, offering an incredibly easy and nutritious meal.

Serving: 6
| Preparation Time: 10 minutes
| Ready Time: 25 minutes

Ingredients:
- 2 cups cooked lentils
- 2 cups diced eggplant
- 2 cups diced red bell pepper
- 2 cups diced onion
- 2 tablespoons olive oil
- 1 tablespoon smoked paprika
- Salt and pepper, to taste
- 2 tablespoons chopped parsley

Instructions:
1. Preheat oven to 425F.
2. Line two baking sheets with parchment paper.
3. Place the diced eggplant, red bell pepper, and onion onto one of the baking sheets.
4. Drizzle the vegetables with olive oil, smoked paprika, salt, and pepper. Toss to coat.
5. Arrange the vegetables on the baking sheet in a single layer and bake for 10 minutes.
6. Meanwhile, heat the cooked lentils on the other baking sheet for 10 minutes.
7. Once the vegetables and lentils are roasted, combine them in a bowl.
8. Sprinkle the chopped parsley over the top of the salad and serve.

Nutrition Information (per serving):
- Calories: 270
- Carbohydrates: 33 g
- Protein: 15 g
- Fat: 9 g
- Saturated Fat: 1 g
- Cholesterol: 0 mg
- Sodium: 230 mg
- Fiber: 9 g

75. Lentil and Kale Burger

This homemade Lentil and Kale Burger is a great healthy alternative to traditional burgers. Packed with protein and nutrition, it makes a delicious and nutritious meal that the whole family will enjoy.

Serving: 6
| Preparation Time: 15 minutes
| Ready Time: 45 minutes

Ingredients:

- 1/2 cup green lentils
- 2 cups water
- 1 tablespoon olive oil
- 1/2 onion, diced
- 2 cloves garlic, minced
- 1 carrot, peeled and grated
- 1 cup cooked kale
- 1/2 cup rolled oats
- 1 teaspoon Worcestershire sauce
- Salt & pepper, to taste
- 6 whole wheat buns

Instructions:

1. In a medium saucepan over high heat, add the lentils, water and a pinch of salt. Bring to a boil, then reduce the heat to low and simmer for 35 minutes, or until the lentils are cooked through.

2. Preheat oven to 350F (175°C). Heat the oil in a pan over medium heat, then add the onion and garlic and sauté until the onion is soft and translucent. Add the carrot, kale, oats and Worcestershire sauce and sauté for another 5 minutes.

3. Add the cooked lentils to the pan and season with salt and pepper. For a smoother texture, use a potato masher to mash the lentils a bit. Stir well and cook for another 5 minutes.

4. Divide the mixture evenly into 6 patties and place on a parchment-lined baking sheet. Bake in the oven for 15 minutes, flipping the patties halfway through.

5. Serve the patties on whole wheat buns with your favorite burger toppings. Enjoy!

Nutrition Information (per serving):

Calories: 210
Fat: 5g

Carbohydrates: 30g
Protein: 10g
Fiber: 5g

76. Grilled Cheese and Egg Sandwich

This classic combination of grilled cheese and egg sandwich is a delicious breakfast or lunch option. Enjoy the flavors of melted cheese, egg, and savory spices in this one-of-a-kind sandwich.
Servings: 2
| Preparation Time: 10 minutes
| Ready Time: 10 minutes

Ingredients:
1.   2 slices white or whole wheat bread
2.   2 tablespoons butter
3.   2 large eggs
4.   salt and pepper to taste
5.   4 slices sharp cheddar cheese

Instructions:
1. Heat a large skillet over medium heat.
2. Spread 1 tablespoon butter on each slice of bread and place butter-side down in the skillet.
3. Crack an egg into each slice of bread and season with salt and pepper.
4. Turn heat to low and cook for about 4 minutes or until eggs are cooked through.
5. Place 2 slices of cheese on the egg.
6. Melt the cheese, then place the second piece of bread on top, butter-side up and cook for 2 minutes, flipping once during cooking.

Nutrition Information:
Calories: 540, Total Fat: 33g, Saturated Fat: 16g, Carbohydrates: 33g, Protein: 27g, Cholesterol: 276mg, Sodium: 708mg, Fiber: 2g.

77. Egg and Veggie Muffin Cups

Egg and Veggie Muffin Cups - These delicious egg and veggie muffin cups are a nutritious and convenient breakfast on the go. They are loaded with broccoli, zucchini, onions, bell peppers, and cheddar cheese, baked in their own individual portion sizes, and best of all, the cups can be frozen and reheated for a later date.

Serving: 12 muffin cups
| Preparation Time: 10 minutes
| Ready Time: 25 minutes

Ingredients:
- 6 eggs
- 1/4 cup milk
- 1/4 cup onion, diced
- 1/4 cup bell pepper, diced
- 1/2 cup cooked broccoli, chopped
- 1/2 cup cooked zucchini, chopped
- 1/2 cup cheddar cheese, shredded
- Salt and pepper

Instructions:
1. Preheat the oven to 375F and grease or line a 12 cup muffin pan with liners.
2. In a medium bowl, whisk together the eggs and milk until blended.
3. Stir in the onion, bell pepper, broccoli, zucchini, and cheddar cheese until well combined.
4. Divide the mixture evenly among the 12 muffin cups.
5. Sprinkle with a little salt and pepper and bake for 20-25 minutes, until golden and cooked through.
6. Let cool for 5 minutes before removing the muffin cups and serve warm.

Nutrition Information:
Per muffin cup; Calories: 77; Fat: 5g; Total Carbs: 1.5g; Protein: 6g; Sodium: 127mg

78. Salmon Salad with Edamame

This bright and flavorful Salmon Salad with Edamame is a delicious meal that can be made quickly, with a perfect balance of Omega-3 fatty acids from the salmon and a satisfying crunch from the edamame.
Serving: 4
| Preparation Time: 10 minutes
| Ready Time: 15 minutes

Ingredients:
- 2 cups cooked salmon (or canned salmon)
- 2 cups frozen edamame
- 2 tablespoons olive oil
- 2 tablespoons fresh lemon juice
- 1/4 teaspoon sea salt
- 1/4 teaspoon freshly ground black pepper

Instructions:
1. Place cooked salmon in a small bowl and mash with a fork
2. In a medium bowl, combine edamame, olive oil, lemon juice, salt, and pepper.
3. Add the mashed salmon to the edamame and stir to combine.
4. Serve in individual bowls and enjoy.

Nutrition Information:
Calories: 152; Total Fat: 7.2 g; Saturated Fat: 1.4 g; Cholesterol: 26 g; Sodium: 125 mg; Carbohydrates: 6.9 g; Fiber: 2 g; Sugar: 0.3 g; Protein: 15.2 g.

79. Hummus and Veggie Wrap

Packed with vegetables and creamy hummus, this delicious and healthy Hummus and Veggie Wrap is easy to make and perfect for lunch or dinner.
Serving: 2
| Preparation Time: 15 minutes
| Ready Time: 15 minutes

Ingredients:
- 2 tortillas

- 2 tablespoons of hummus
- 1/2 cup diced bell peppers
- 1/2 cup thinly sliced carrots
- 1/2 cup shredded lettuce
- 1/4 cup diced cucumbers

Instructions:
1. Spread 1 tablespoon of hummus over each tortilla.
2. Place bell peppers, carrots, lettuce, and cucumbers over the hummus.
3. Roll the tortillas up and slice in half before serving.

Nutrition Information:
Calories: 130 kcal, Carbohydrates: 18 g, Protein: 4 g, Fat: 4 g, Saturated
Fat: 1 g, Sodium: 240 mg, Potassium: 132 mg, Fiber: 3 g, Sugar: 2 g,
Vitamin A: 54.9%, Vitamin C: 46.5%, Calcium: 2.8%, Iron: 7.1%

80. Burrito Bowl with Cauliflower Rice

Burrito Bowl with Cauliflower Rice is a tasty and healthy meal packed
with flavorsome ingredients and nutrients. It's a great option for meat-
free and low-carb diets. Serve it for lunch or dinner—or both!
Serving: 4
| Preparation Time: 10 minutes
| Ready Time: 15 minutes

Ingredients:
1.   1 head of cauliflower
2.   2-3 tablespoons extra-virgin olive oil
3.   1 onion, diced
4.   1 red bell pepper, diced
5.   2 cloves of garlic, minced
6.   1 cup corn kernels
7.   1 can black beans, drained and rinsed
8.   1/2 teaspoon cumin
9.   1/4 teaspoon chili powder
10. 1/4 teaspoon paprika
11. 1/4 teaspoon garlic powder
12. 1/4 teaspoon onion powder

13. 1/4 teaspoon salt
14. 1/4 teaspoon black pepper
15. 2 roma tomatoes, diced
16. 1/4 cup fresh coriander, chopped

Instructions:
1. Preheat your oven to 400F.
2. Break or cut cauliflower into florets and pulse in a food processor or grate with a cheese grater until it resembles rice.
3. Spread out on baking sheet, drizzle with olive oil, and bake for 8-10 minutes, or until cauliflower is golden and crispy.
4. Meanwhile, heat 1 tablespoon of olive oil in a large skillet over medium heat.
5. Add in onion and red bell pepper. Stir and cook until softened, about 6 minutes.
6. Add in garlic and corn, stirring for about two minutes.
7. Add in beans, cumin, chili powder, paprika, garlic powder, onion powder, salt, and black pepper. Stir and cook for about five minutes.
8. Stir in diced tomatoes. Saute for two minutes.
9. To assemble, spoon cauliflower rice into a bowl and top with beans mixture and fresh cilantro.

Nutrition Information:
Calories: 207
Total Fat: 7 g
Saturated Fat: 1 g
Cholesterol: 0 mg
Sodium: 382 mg
Carbohydrates: 30 g
Fiber: 8 g
Sugar: 6 g
Protein: 9 g

81. Greek Salad with Chicken

Greek Salad with Chicken is a zesty combination of crisp salad greens and hearty protein. Succulent grilled chicken breast, sliced tomatoes and cucumber, Kalamata olives, red onion, and feta cheese are tossed together with a full-bodied Greek vinaigrette. It's a tasty, rustic concoction, lightweight in texture and rich in flavor.

Serving: 6-8
| Preparation Time: 15 minutes
| Ready Time: 15 minutes

Ingredients:
- 2 boneless chicken breasts
- 1 head romaine lettuce, chopped
- 2 tomatoes, diced
- 1 cucumber, peeled and sliced
- 1 red onion, thinly sliced
- 1/2 cup feta cheese
- 1/2 cup kalamata olives, pitted
- 2 tablespoons olive oil
- 2 tablespoons red wine vinegar
- 1 tablespoon lemon juice
- 2 teaspoons dried oregano
- Salt and pepper, to taste

Instructions:
1. Begin by preheating an outdoor grill, or indoor grill pan to medium-high heat.
2. Season the chicken breasts with salt and pepper, and cook on the grill until the outside is nicely charred and the chicken is cooked through, about 7 minutes per side. Once cooked through, set aside to cool slightly and then slice into strips.
3. In a large salad bowl, combine the lettuce, tomatoes, cucumber, red onion, feta cheese, and olives.
4. In a separate bowl, whisk together the olive oil, red wine vinegar, lemon juice, oregano, salt, and pepper. Pour over the salad and toss to combine.
5. Top the salad with the grilled chicken strips and serve.

Nutrition Information:
Per Serving:
Calories - 294
Fat - 13g
Carbohydrates - 15g
Protein - 28g

Sodium - 325mg

82. Avocado and Egg Toast

Avocado and Egg Toast is a delicious and nutritious breakfast, lunch, or light dinner option. Perfect for when you need something easy and healthy. This dish is easy to make and will leave your tastebuds wanting more.
Serving: 1 person, | Preparation Time: 5 minutes, | Ready Time: 10 minutes.

Ingredients:
1. 2 pieces of whole wheat toast,
2. 1 ripe avocado,
3. 2 eggs,
4. salt,
5. pepper.

Instructions:
1. Bring a small saucepan of water to a boil and gently add the eggs, simmer for 5 minutes.
2. Toast your bread while the eggs are cooking and cut the avocado into slices.
3. Once the eggs are cooked, peel them and place them on the toast.
4. Top with the sliced avocado and sprinkle with salt and pepper.

Nutrition Information:
413 calories, 24 g fat, 39 g carbohydrates, 12 g protein.

83. Quinoa Veggie Bowl

Quinoa Veggie Bowl is a hearty and healthy vegetarian meal that is easy to make, packed with protein and full of flavor.
Serving: 4
| Preparation Time: 10 Minutes
| Ready Time: 30 Minutes

Ingredients:
- 2 cups of cooked quinoa
- 2 large carrots, grated
- 1 red onion, finely chopped
- 2 cloves garlic, minced
- 2 tablespoons olive oil
- 500 grams mushrooms, chopped
- 2 tablespoons thyme
- 2 large bell peppers, diced
- 1 zucchini, diced
- 1 can of chickpeas, drained and rinsed
- 2 tablespoons tahini
- 2 tablespoons lemon juice
- Salt and pepper to taste

Instructions:
1. Preheat the oven to 375F.
2. In a bowl, mix together the quinoa, carrots, red onion, garlic, olive oil, mushrooms, thyme, bell peppers, and zucchini.
3. Spread the mixture onto a baking sheet and bake for 25-30 minutes, stirring occasionally, until vegetables have softened and golden.
4. In a medium bowl, whisk together the tahini and lemon juice.
5. Add the chickpeas and cooked quinoa mixture to the bowl and stir to combine.
6. Season to taste with salt and pepper.
7. Serve in bowls topped with extra lemon juice, tahini, and fresh herbs.

Nutrition Information (per serving):
Calories: 370
Total Fat: 12g
Saturated Fat: 2g
Carbohydrates: 56g
Fiber: 12g
Protein: 11g
Sodium: 157mg

84. Chickpea Curry with Brown Rice

This chickpea curry with brown rice dish is both satisfying and nutritious. It is packed with heart-healthy whole grains, protein-rich chickpeas, and antioxidant-rich spices. It also features a flavor punch from a medley of spices and a creamy thickness from coconut milk.
Serving: 4
| Preparation Time: 10 minutes
| Ready Time: 35 minutes

Ingredients:
- 2 tablespoons olive oil
- 2 teaspoons cumin
- 1 teaspoon turmeric
- 2 cloves garlic, minced
- 1 large onion, diced
- 3 cups cooked chickpeas
- 1 cup canned crushed tomatoes
- 1/2 teaspoon chili powder
- 1/4 teaspoon sea salt + more to taste
- 2 cups broth
- 1/2 cup canned full-fat coconut milk
- 2 cups cooked brown rice
- Fresh parsley or cilantro, for garnish

Instructions:
1. Heat oil in a large pot over medium heat. Add the cumin, turmeric, garlic, and onion and cook, stirring occasionally until the vegetables are softened, about 6 minutes.
2. Add the chickpeas, crushed tomatoes, chili powder, and salt and stir to combine.
3. Pour in the broth and coconut milk and bring to a simmer. Simmer, uncovered, for 15 minutes, stirring occasionally.
4. Serve the curry spooned over the cooked brown rice and garnish with chopped fresh herbs.

Nutrition Information:
Calories 188, Fat 6g, Protein 7g, Carbs 29g, Fiber 8g, Sugars 3g.

85. Grilled Chicken with Pesto

This quick and easy Grilled Chicken with Pesto makes a delicious dinner that is prepared in no time and will be sure to please any palate.
Serving: 4 servings
| Preparation Time: 20 minutes
| Ready Time: 25 minutes

Ingredients:
- 4 boneless chicken breasts
- 1/4 cup prepared pesto
- 1/4 cup olive oil
- Salt and pepper
- 2 cloves garlic, minced
- 1/4 cup grated Parmesan cheese

Instructions:
1. Preheat grill to medium heat.
2. Place chicken breasts in a shallow dish or bowl.
3. In a small bowl, mix together pesto, olive oil, garlic, salt and pepper, and Parmesan cheese.
4. Spread pesto mixture over the chicken breasts.
5. Grill the chicken for 4 to 6 minutes per side, or until the chicken is cooked through and the pesto is slightly charred.
6. Serve chicken with additional Parmesan cheese and garnish with fresh herbs, if desired.

Nutrition Information:
Per serving: 262 calories, 15.5 g fat, 5.8 g carbohydrate, 17.9 g protein

86. Cottage Cheese and Capers Salad

Cottage Cheese and Capers Salad is a tasty and healthy twist on a classic salad. Full of flavor and nutrition, this salad makes a great side dish or entrée for lunch or dinner.
Serves 4, | Preparation Time 15 mins, Ready in 15 mins.

Ingredients:

1. 4 cups red leaf lettuce, torn
2. 2 cups skim cottage cheese
3. 2 tablespoons lemon juice
4. 2 tablespoons drained capers
5. 2 tablespoons olive oil
6. 1 tablespoon minced fresh parsley

Instructions:
1. In a large bowl, combine the lettuce, cottage cheese, lemon juice, capers and parsley.
2. Drizzle the olive oil over the salad and mix the ingredients together until evenly combined.

Nutrition Information:
Calories: 149.3
Protein: 12.3g
Carbs: 4.4g
Fat: 8.4g

87. Tuna Salad with Avocado

Tuna Salad with Avocado is a hearty and healthy lunch or light dinner perfect for any day. It's easy to make and full of flavor!
Serving: 4
| Preparation Time: 10 minutes
| Ready Time: 10 minutes

Ingredients:
- 2 cans wild light tuna in water, drained
- 2 stalks celery, diced
- 1/2 small red onion, diced
- 1 large ripe avocado, diced
- 1/4 cup plain greek yogurt
- 1 tablespoon mayonnaise
- 1 tablespoon dill relish
- Juice of 1 lemon
- Salt and pepper to taste

Instructions:
1. In a large bowl, combine tuna, celery, red onion and avocado.
2. In a small bowl, mix together yogurt, mayonnaise, relish and lemon juice.
3. Pour dressing over tuna mixture and season with salt and pepper, to taste.
4. Serve chilled.

Nutrition Information:
Per serving: Calories 210, Protein 18g, Carbohydrate 8g, Sugar 2.6g, Fiber 4g, Fat 11g, Cholesterol 24mg, Sodium 508mg.

88. Broccoli and Prosciutto Quiche

This Broccoli and Prosciutto Quiche is a savory, delicious main dish that's perfect for any special occasion or an easy weeknight dinner. Serves 8, | Preparation Time 10 minutes, Ready time between 45 minutes.

Ingredients:
- 1 refrigerated pie crust
- 1/4 cup extra-virgin olive oil
- 1 medium onion, chopped
- 6 prosciutto slices, chopped
- 2 cloves garlic, minced
- 2 cups pre-cooked broccoli
- 4 large eggs
- 1 1/2 cups milk
- 1/2 teaspoon salt
- 1/4 teaspoon black pepper
- 1/2 cup shredded Swiss cheese

Instructions:
1. Preheat oven to 400F.
2. Unroll and fit the pie crust into a 9-inch pie plate and flute the edges. Set aside.

3. In a large skillet, heat the olive oil over medium heat. Add the onions and prosciutto and cook, stirring occasionally for about 5 minutes, until the onions are softened.

4. Add the garlic and cook for an additional 1 minute. Remove the skillet from the heat and set aside.

5. Spread the pre-cooked broccoli in the prepared pie crust.

6. In a medium bowl, whisk together the eggs, milk, salt, and pepper.

7. Pour the egg mixture into the pie crust, over the broccoli.

8. Top with the onion and prosciutto mixture and the shredded cheese.

9. Bake for 45 minutes, or until the top is golden brown, and a knife inserted into the center comes out clean.

10. Let cool slightly before serving.

Nutrition Information:
Calories: 285, Total Fat: 18 g, Saturated Fat: 7 g, Cholesterol: 116 mg, Sodium: 837 mg, Total Carbohydrate: 17 g, Dietary Fiber: 2 g, Protein: 13 g

89. Spicy Tofu Burrito Bowl

A flavorful Spicy Tofu Burrito Bowl that is the perfect combination of healthy and delicious! Packed with plant-based proteins, grains and veggies, this bowl is sure to please those with vegetarian, vegan and meat-eater diets.

Serves: 4 | | Preparation Time: 10 mins | | Ready Time: 20 mins

Ingredients:
-14oz extra firm tofu
-3 tablespoons olive oil
-1 teaspoon chili powder
-1 teaspoon garlic powder
-1 teaspoon smoked paprika
-1 teaspoon cumin
-1 teaspoon sea salt
-1 cup cooked short grain brown rice
-2 bell peppers, diced
-1/2 red onion, diced
-1/2 cup canned black beans, drained and rinsed

-1/2 cup fresh salsa
-1/4 cup fresh cilantro, chopped
-2 avocados, sliced
-Optional: hot sauce

Instructions:
1. Preheat oven to 375F. Line baking sheet with parchment paper.
2. In a large mixing bowl, combine tofu, olive oil, chili powder, garlic powder, smoked paprika, cumin and sea salt. Mix until the tofu is evenly coated.
3. Transfer the tofu to the parchment lined baking sheet and bake for 15 minutes.
4. While tofu is baking, prepare the bell peppers, red onion and black beans by placing them into a large bowl.
5. When the tofu is done baking, add it to the bowl with the bell peppers, red onion and black beans.
6. To assemble the burrito bowls, divide the rice, salsa, cilantro and avocado between 4 bowls. Top each bowl with the spicy tofu mixture.
7. Serve with hot sauce, if desired.

Nutrition Information:
One serving of Spicy Tofu Burrito Bowl contains 486 calories, 25.2 g total fat, 6.2 g saturated fat, 464 mg sodium, 49.7 g carbohydrates, 10.1 g dietary fiber, 10.2 g sugar, and 21.2 g protein.

90. Egg Muffins with Vegetables

Egg Muffins with Vegetables is a delicious and healthy recipe that is quick and easy to make. This recipe yields 12 servings, takes 15 minutes to prepare and is ready in 25 minutes.

Ingredients:
- 12 eggs
- 1/2 cup grated cheese
- 1/2 cup red pepper, chopped
- 1/2 cup mushrooms, chopped
- 1/4 cup red onion, chopped
- 1/4 teaspoon salt

- Non-stick cooking spray

Instructions:
1. Preheat oven to 375F.
2. Spray a 12-cup muffin tin with cooking spray.
3. In a large bowl, whisk together the eggs and grated cheese.
4. Add in the red pepper, mushrooms, red onion, and salt.
5. Divide the mixture evenly among the 12 muffin cups.
6. Bake for 20-25 minutes, or until the eggs are set.

Nutrition Information per serving:
Calories 110, Total Fat 7g, Saturated Fat 3g, Cholesterol 195mg, Sodium 270mg, Carbohydrate 2g, Protein 9g.

91. Peanut Butter and Protein Balls

Peanut Butter and Protein Balls are a delicious and nutritious snack that can be enjoyed as breakfast, a pre-workout snack, or a sweet after-dinner treat. Packed with protein, fiber, and healthy fats, these yummy balls will keep you feeling satiated.
Serving: Makes 12 balls
| Preparation Time: 10 minutes
| Ready Time: 1 hour

Ingredients:
- 1 cup peanut butter
- 1 scoop of your favorite protein powder
- 2 tablespoons coconut oil, melted
- 1/4 cup honey
- 1/4 cup almond flour
- 1/4 cup ground flax seed

Instructions:
1. Place all the ingredients in a medium-sized bowl.
2. Mix until everything is fully combined and the batter turns into a thick paste.
3. Wet your hands and roll 12 walnut-sized balls and set aside on parchment paper.

4. Place the protein balls in the refrigerator for one hour.

Nutrition Information (per serving):
Calories: 166
Fat: 11 g
Carbohydrates: 12 g
Protein: 6 g

92. Greek Yogurt and Fruit Parfait

Greek Yogurt and Fruit Parfait is a delicious and healthy breakfast or snack. It's a simple no-cook meal that can be prepped ahead and assembled quickly. With the fresh flavors of Greek yogurt, granola, and fresh fruit, this easy parfait makes a great start to the day.
Serving: 4
| Preparation Time: 10 minutes
| Ready Time: 10 minutes

Ingredients:
-1 cup of Greek yogurt
-1/2 cup of granola
-1/2 cup of fresh berries
-1/2 cup of diced apples
-1 tablespoon of honey

Instructions:
1. Divide yogurt into four small glass containers or parfait glasses.
2. Top each glass of yogurt with 1/4 cup of granola.
3. Top the granola with an equal amount of berries and diced apples.
4. Drizzle a tablespoon of honey over the fruit in each container.
5. Give each glass one final stir and serve.

Nutrition Information:
Calories: 212
Total fat: 5g
Saturated fat: 1g
Trans fat: 0g
Cholesterol: 0mg

Sodium: 78mg
Carbohydrates: 32g
Fiber: 4g
Sugar: 22g
Protein: 10g

93. Salad Nicoise with Grilled Salmon

Salad Nicoise with Grilled Salmon is an easy and delicious meal for any occasion. Rich and savory, this dish features fresh ingredients with a simple preparation process that yields wholesome and flavorful results. Serves 4. | Preparation Time: 15 minutes. | Ready Time: 15 minutes.

Ingredients:
- 4 salmon fillets (4 ounces each)
- 1 pound new potatoes, halved
- 2 tablespoons olive oil, divided
- 2 cloves garlic, minced
- Kosher salt and freshly ground black pepper, to taste
- 2 large eggs
- 2 heads butter lettuce, leaves separated
- 2 large tomatoes, diced
- 1/4 cup black olives, pitted and halved
- 4 anchovy fillets
- 4 tablespoons chopped fresh parsley, divided
- 2 tablespoons freshly squeezed lemon juice

Instructions:
1. Preheat oven to 400F.
2. Place potatoes on a baking sheet and toss with 1 tablespoon olive oil. Season with garlic, salt and pepper, to taste. Roast potatoes for 12-15 minutes, or until tender.
3. Heat remaining 1 tablespoon olive oil in a large skillet over medium high heat. Sear salmon for 2-3 minutes per side, or until cooked through.
4. Meanwhile, hard-boil eggs. Place eggs in a saucepan and cover with cold water. Bring to a boil and cook for 7 minutes, then plunge into cold water. Peel and dice eggs.

5. To assemble salad, combine lettuce, diced tomatoes, cooked potatoes, eggs, olives, anchovies and 3 tablespoons parsley in a large bowl. Drizzle with lemon juice and remaining 1 tablespoon parsley. Gently toss to combine.

6. Divide salad among four plates and top each with one salmon fillet before serving.

Nutrition Information:
Calories: 293, Protein: 17.2g, Total Fat: 11.8g, Carbohydrates: 22.2g, Cholesterol: 121.8mg, Sodium: 412.1mg, Sugars: 2.8g, Fiber: 2.6g

94. Southwestern Egg Scramble

Southwestern Egg Scramble is an easy, savory breakfast packed with flavor from roasted chiles, fresh tomatoes, and onions. A simple blend of Tex-Mex spices adds a burst of flavor, great for any morning!
Serves 8. | Preparation Time: 10 minutes; | Ready Time: 10 minutes.

Ingredients:
- 8 large eggs
- 2 tablespoons butter
- 1/2 cup diced onion
- 1 cup roasted chile peppers (such as Hatch or Poblano), diced
- 1 cup diced tomatoes
- 1 teaspoon ground cumin
- 1 teaspoon smoked paprika
- Salt and freshly ground black pepper, to taste

Instructions:
1. In a large bowl, whisk together the eggs until well combined.
2. In a large frying pan over medium-high heat, melt the butter. Add the onion and cook, stirring often, until softened, about 4 minutes.
3. Add the chiles, tomatoes, cumin, and smoked paprika. Cook until the vegetables are heated through and softened, about 2 minutes.
4. Pour the egg mixture over the vegetables. Cook, stirring constantly, until just set, about 2 minutes.
5. Season with salt and pepper, and serve.

Nutrition Information (per serving):
Calories: 136; Total Fat: 9g; Cholesterol: 191mg; Sodium: 133mg; Total
Carbohydrate: 4g; Protein: 9g.

95. Tofu and Carrot Lettuce Wraps

Tofu and Carrot Lettuce Wraps are a delicious and healthy lunch or
dinner option providing a flavorful combination of protein and
vegetables. With just 15 minutes of | Preparation Time and 5 minutes of
cook time, this light and refreshing dish can be enjoyed in no time at all!
Serving: 4
| Preparation Time: 15 minutes
| Ready Time: 20 minutes

Ingredients:
- 1 tablespoon olive oil
- 1 block of extra firm tofu, cubed
- 1 large carrot, shredded
- 2 tablespoons fresh parsley, chopped
- Salt and black pepper to taste
- 4 large lettuce leaves
- 2 tablespoons sesame seeds, toasted

Instructions:
1. Heat the oil in a large skillet over medium-high heat.
2. Add the cubed tofu and cook for about 5 minutes until tofu is lightly
browned, stirring occasionally.
3. Add the shredded carrot and parsley and season with salt and pepper.
Cook for an additional 2-3 minutes.
4. Remove skillet from heat and spoon the mixture into lettuce leaves.
5. Garnish with sesame seeds and serve.

Nutrition Information (per serving):
Calories: 184, Total Fat: 11g, Saturated Fat: 2g, Cholesterol: 0mg,
Sodium: 16mg, Carbohydrates: 11g, Fiber: 3g, Protein: 10g.

96. Protein Pancakes

Protein Pancakes are a delicious and healthy way to start your day. Packed with eggs, oats, and cottage cheese, these pancakes are sure to give you a protein boost and keep you feeling energetic all morning!
Serving: 8-10 pancakes
| Preparation Time: 8 minutes
| Ready Time: 15 minutes

Ingredients:
• 4 eggs
• 2 cups oats
• 1/2 cup cottage cheese
• 2 tablespoons coconut flour
• 2 teaspoons baking powder
• 1 teaspoon baking soda
• Pinch of salt

Instructions:
1. In a blender, combine eggs, oats, and cottage cheese. Blend on high until a smooth batter forms.
2. Add coconut flour, baking powder, baking soda, and salt to the blender and mix until everything is well combined.
3. Heat a large skillet to medium heat and coat with a thin layer of oil.
4. Ladle 1/4 cup pancake batter onto the hot skillet and cook for about 2-3 minutes on each side, or until golden brown.
5. Serve with your favorite toppings and enjoy!

Nutrition Information:
Calories: 290, Fat: 7 g, Carbs: 25 g, Protein: 23 g

97. Grilled Turkey and Vegetables

Grilled Turkey and Vegetables is an easy, healthy and flavorful dinner that your whole family will love. Served with a simple side salad, it is a great way to summon warm summer evenings.
Serving: 4
| Preparation Time: 10 minutes

| Ready Time: 40 minutes

Ingredients:
- 2-3 boneless turkey breasts
- 1 bell pepper
- 1 zucchini
- 1 red onion
- 2 tablespoons olive oil
- 2 tablespoons lemon juice
- 1 teaspoon ground black pepper
- 1 tablespoon chopped mixed herbs (e.g. parsley, oregano, basil)

Instructions:
1. Preheat a grill to medium-high heat.
2. Cut the bell pepper, zucchini and red onion into thick slices.
3. Place the turkey breast in plastic wrap and use a mallet or rolling pin to make thin slices.
4. Toss the pepper, onion and zucchini in a large bowl with the olive oil, lemon juice, black pepper and herbs.
5. Grill the poultry until it is cooked through (reaching an internal temperature of 165F).
6. Place the vegetables alongside the turkey on the grill and cook for about 6-7 minutes.
7. Serve the turkey and vegetables hot.

Nutrition Information:
Calories: 304; Protein: 36g; Total Fat: 11g; Carbohydrate: 9g; Dietary Fiber: 2g; Sodium: 90mg

98. Roasted Veggie, Lentil and Feta Salad

Roasted Veggie, Lentil and Feta Salad is a delicious, nutritious, vegan-friendly dish. It is full of rich flavors, making it a perfect healthy meal or snack.
Serves 4, Prep Time 10 minutes, Ready Time 25 minutes.

Ingredients:
-1 red onion, cut into wedges

-2 carrots, cut into chunks
-2 red peppers, cut into 1-inch pieces
-2 zucchini, sliced into 1-inch rounds
-3 tablespoons olive oil
-1/2 cup dry green lentils, rinsed
-1/2 teaspoon salt
-1/4 cup white wine vinegar
-2 tablespoons Dijon mustard
-2 tablespoons honey
-4 ounces of feta cheese, crumbled

Instructions:
1. Preheat oven to 400F.
2. Line a rimmed baking sheet with parchment paper.
3. Arrange the onion, carrots, red peppers, and zucchini onto the prepared baking sheet and drizzle with the olive oil.
4. Roast in the preheated oven for 20-25 minutes or until golden and tender.
5. Meanwhile, bring 2 cups of water to a boil in a medium saucepan. Add the lentils and salt, reduce heat to low and simmer uncovered for 15-20 minutes or until lentils are tender. Drain any remaining liquid and set aside.
6. While the vegetables and lentils are cooking, prepare the dressing by combining the vinegar, mustard, and honey in a small bowl.
7. When everything is done cooking, combine the roasted vegetables, lentils, and dressing in a large bowl and toss to combine.
8. Sprinkle with feta cheese and serve.

Nutrition Information (1 serving):
Calories 223 Total Fat 12.4g Cholesterol 18mg Sodium 447mg
Carbohydrates 21.4g Sugars 6.5g Protein 9.1g

CONCLUSION

When it comes to quick and delicious meals that also provide high protein intake, the 98 High-Protein Lunches cookbook has you covered. With a variety of healthy, protein-rich recipes, this collection of recipes makes it easy to enjoy a nutritious and balanced meal while on-the-go. Whether you're a full-time worker, a stay-at-home parent, or a busy college student, the recipes in this cookbook can help you pack the protein you need into your morning, lunch and dinner.

The meals in this cookbook are made to be easily adaptable to individual dietary needs and tastes – for example, you can substitute vegetarian ingredients for animal proteins, gluten-free grains for wheat, and dairy-free products for milk-based ones. If you're looking for a way to get the protein you need without sacrificing delicious flavors, this cookbook is a great way to start.

Whether you're meal prepping or just throwing together a quick lunch, these recipes make it easy to add healthy, protein-packed lunches to your weekly lineup. From classic favorites to creative twists on traditional dishes, 98 High-Protein Lunches offers a balancing act between fast and flavorful. For busy bodies seeking a high-protein solution, this cookbook is the perfect addition to any kitchen. With its simple instructions, wide selection of recipes and accommodations for dietary restrictions, 98 High-Protein Lunches creates a foundation of nutrition and taste that leaves no craving unsatisfied.

Printed in Great Britain
by Amazon

57410172R00059